The **RYA** Book

Buying Your First Motor Cruiser

Robert Avis

ADLARD COLES NAUTICAL
London

To my very best friend
who now knows far more
about buying her first
motor cruiser than she ever
really wanted to know!

Published 2000 by Adlard Coles Nautical
an imprint of A & C Black (Publishers) Ltd
35 Bedford Row, London WC1R 4JH
www.adlardcoles.co.uk

ISBN 0–7136–5074-5

The author, Robert Avis, has asserted his right under
the Copyright, Designs and Patents Act, 1988, to be
identified as the author of this work.

A CIP catalogue record for this book is available
from the British Library.

Note: While all reasonable care has been taken in
the preparation of this book, the publisher takes no
responsibility for the use of the methods or products
or contracts described in the book.

Typeset in 10 on 12pt Concorde Regular
Printed and bound in Great Britain by
The Cromwell Press, Trowbridge, Wiltshire

Contents

Introduction

'. . . Believe me, my young friend, there is nothing – absolutely nothing - half so much worth doing as simply messing about in boats. . .'

I am certain that when Kenneth Grahame wrote that immortal line for the Water Rat in 1908 he could not possibly have begun to conceive how popular 'messing about in boats' was likely to become over the ensuing ninety years or so.

Nowadays more than ten per cent of our adult population spend some part of their leisure time in their own boats: racing or just cruising around and a further eight per cent of non-boat owners, have a keen interest in maritime pursuits. It is hardly surprising, therefore, that by satisfying a growing and discerning home market, British boat and marine equipment manufacturers have become world leaders. Almost sixty per cent of British production is now exported adding over £300 million to our delicate balance of trade surplus.

As an island nation which has developed over thousands of years, we must all have been born with a little bit of sea water in our veins, but what is it that makes us take to the water? I suspect it is curiosity. It is well known that mariners are very curious people and there is nothing more fascinating than the sea. It is never the same for two consecutive days, it is totally beyond control, it has incredible power and it warrants the greatest respect.

So how do people get into motor boating? The majority start either as children with enthusiastic boating parents, or with friends, or by a charter holiday. I grew up with parents who were terribly keen on the idea of boating holidays but with no real experience in the early days. I soon discovered, as a youngster, that all our family holidays were to be boating holidays with the inevitable nautical mishaps and hilarity that followed! We pottered around the Solent, progressing later to our first cross-Channel crossing to Cherbourg – this gave us a real sense of navigational achievement even if we did miss Cherbourg at the first attempt! In those days we didn't have GPS, and long-hand navigation really was the only way.

The Channel Islands and Brittany came next as confidence grew and, over the years, our boats got larger and larger to cope with an ever increasing family! Soon we were heading west to Devon and Cornwall and a year later it was to be east to Belgium and Holland. One of our most memorable holidays was to cruise across the Channel and up the River Seine to Paris. There is something very special about mooring up within sight of the Eiffel Tower and Notre Dame. In fact I thought that it was so special that I even managed to persuade my fiancée that Paris was the place to honeymoon; but unfortunately my romantic notion of cruising across there by boat went down like the proverbial lead balloon!

Robert Avis

Acknowledgements

Books of this nature are rarely compiled from a single source, so I should like to offer my sincere thanks to the following who have guided me through some of the more intricate and less well-known technical and legal aspects of buying a motor cruiser.

Bill Anderson, RYA Training Manager
Association of Brokers & Yacht Agents
British Marine Industries Federation
Caroline Brookes, Boatmark Ltd
Carole Edwards, editor Adlard Coles
    Nautical
Carol Fowler, Editor RYA Magazine

Richard Gould, WG Insurance
HM Customs & Excise, Southampton
Paul Lemmer, Inflatable Boats
    International
Sue McKichan, Marina Developments Ltd
Mike Oram, Dover Sea School
John Puddifoot, Capital Training
Bill Rea, Rea Associates
Registry of Shipping and Seamen, Cardiff
Duncan Saunders, Yacht Services
    International
Robin Sjoberg, RYA Cruising Manager
Edmund Whelan, RYA Legal and
    Government Affairs Manager
Yacht Designers and Surveyors Association

1

What do You Really Want From Your First Boat?

Owning a boat has often been likened to standing in a cold shower tearing up fifty pound notes. If that is your view of boat owning then there is probably not much point in reading any further. There is no doubt that boating is not a cheap hobby but it can provide an interest, a fascination and a satisfaction to which few other pastimes even come close.

If you are planning to buy a boat as part of a family venture, then it is important that the family as a whole are involved in the project right from the very beginning. There have been numerous family men who have visited a boat show, got the boating bug and committed themselves to a considerable investment only to discover, on the first outing, that the family suffer from collective water phobia.

Don't smile, it happens surprisingly often.

An interesting question is why are there so many yachts and motor cruisers tied up in marinas apparently for the whole year? On a recent visit to one of the River Hamble Marinas, a berthing master told me that only 20 per cent of his mooring holders use their boats more than once a month and that over 40 per cent move less than twice a year. Why is this, do you suppose?

Well I have a theory about this. I think that many people who are new to boating, assume that driving a motor cruiser is just like driving a car. (Well take it from me, it isn't, it really isn't. It is much more like driving a double decker bus without brakes on a skid pan.)

The new skipper piles his family on board and confidently heads out of the

Have you been boating before?

It is surprising how many people buy a boat with no previous experience at all. They get a whim, and before reasoned thought has a chance to evaluate the facts, they have committed themselves to a serious investment. Other potential owners are very methodical and attend an introductory RYA training course to give them some background information before venturing forth for the first time and then later supplement their own experience

with more advanced instruction. Some people start boating with a friend and learn the basics that way. This usually works really well if the friend knows what he or she is doing but the difficulty always, as a newcomer to the sport, is trying to gauge the skill of your mentor. Your friend will certainly value a willing pair of hands and, if he has been boating for a few years, he will have a wealth of experience or a host of disasters to share with you.

harbour towards the sparkling sea only to creep back later having perhaps encountered more weather than he can handle or perhaps limping in with some kind of mechanical failure. The family are disillusioned and perhaps even frightened by the experience. Having told all his friends about his super new cruiser, our novice skipper is reluctant to admit that the first outing was less than successful and that his family have refused to go out again. His only option is to keep the boat tied up and go down every so often to give her a wash and to have a few drinks and perhaps spend the odd night aboard. You spend the next two to three years kidding everyone that it was never your intention to go out very often and after that period of time it is reasonable to tell them that you've no longer got the time for boating and have reluctantly decided to sell.

That is my theory as to why so many boats sit glued to the pontoon from one year to the next. I may be wrong but I don't think so.

The way to ensure that this sad scenario does not relate to you is to get some boating experience in advance with friends or with a local club, or at the very least, get a qualified RYA instructor to come out with you on your first few outings to ensure that you and your family or regular crew all get involved and become familiar with this new concept. You can learn a tremendous amount from an experienced instructor and you will soon realise that, no matter how good a boat handler you are, if your crew don't know what they are doing, a technically brilliant approach to your berth can soon turn into the nightmare from hell in a strong breeze with a sluicing tidal stream. Whilst you attempt to scream instructions at your crew, they all run around like headless chickens not knowing what to do. We've all seen it happen, but with proper tuition and plenty of practice with your crew it shouldn't happen to you.

What type of boat might suit you? What are the options?

Boats come in all sorts of shapes and sizes and if you have accepted that the boating bug has bitten, then you have the most difficult task of deciding where to begin. The term 'motor cruiser' suggests to me the option of being able to sleep on board so, for the purposes of this book, I am restricting myself to the purchase of a first motor cruiser with overnight accommodation and cooking facilities. Although this rules out most sports boats, much of the advice given will be equally applicable.

If the adrenalin rush of speed is what you seek then there is a vast selection of new sports boats and even more to choose from on the second-hand market. The sports boat or speed boat starts off at around 3.5m (11.5ft) in length with a 30-40hp outboard and prices from around £2,000. Top speed will be 18-30 knots (nautical miles per hour). This will be fast enough to water ski behind but small enough to tow with the average saloon car. Sports boats up to about 7.5m (24.6ft) and 750-1,000kg gross weight are easily towed. Once you get over this size, a 4x4 vehicle is recommended. And remember that, just because your car may have traction control, you may find that it does not work in reverse as I discovered the other day, trying to reverse my RIB up a slope on a slippery surface and couldn't understand why one wheel kept slipping despite having traction control engaged. In the end I had to borrow a 4x4 to complete the job.

You may feel that leisurely cruising around the waterways of the UK is more your kind of thing. In which case accommodation and comfort will come at the top of the priorities with power and speed well down the list. There are many excellent river cruisers with roomy interiors and small economical engines.

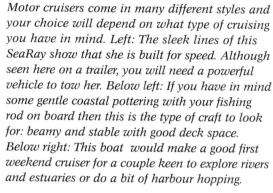

Motor cruisers come in many different styles and your choice will depend on what type of cruising you have in mind. Left: The sleek lines of this SeaRay show that she is built for speed. Although seen here on a trailer, you will need a powerful vehicle to tow her. Below left: If you have in mind some gentle coastal pottering with your fishing rod on board then this is the type of craft to look for: beamy and stable with good deck space. Below right: This boat would make a good first weekend cruiser for a couple keen to explore rivers and estuaries or do a bit of harbour hopping.

Don't assume that a second-hand boat tied up on a river or canal is purely a river boat. Many very seaworthy boats end up on inland waterways as their long-time owners get older and seek a quieter life. When they are eventually sold, they often migrate back to sea with their new owners and start all over again. As a guide, high-powered diesel engined boats were probably originally built for sea-going.

The canals of Europe make really beautiful cruising grounds. You will need a boat sufficiently seaworthy to cross the English Channel but still narrow enough and low enough to negotiate European locks and bridges. Holland is a particularly user-friendly country with its wide locks and many lifting bridges. Bear in mind that other European countries may not be so easy if you have a boat with a flybridge or air draught of more than 3.5m (11.5ft) and want to venture off the main commercial canal routes.

If you want to go further afield, then seaworthiness will be most important and don't forget cruising range. Something you will learn quickly is that sufficient fuel capacity for long passages is vital for a happy time otherwise you will spend your cruising life worrying whether the fuel is going to last to the end of the trip when your attention should be on other things, like navigation perhaps.

Whatever type of cruising you choose to do, take your time and don't rush into a purchase that you might regret later.

If you are planning to cruise on inland waters abroad you will need, as a minimum, an International Certificate of Competence (ICC) which can be taken as a one or two day course (depending upon your experience) at most RYA Recognised Teaching Establishments. See Chapter 11 and Appendix 8.

This elegant, beautifully maintained 52ft displacement motor boat, lying at anchor in Majorca, will cruise at around 10 knots.

Get to the bottom of it: hull types

The intended use of your new boat will determine the type of hull you should be looking for. There are three main types.

Displacement

The first and most traditional is the displacement hull. This is generally a substantial, heavily built, round-bottomed craft which has a maximum hull speed determined by its waterline length. The longer the waterline, the faster the hull will go through the water. At full speed, the whole of the underwater section of the hull remains in the water. Most displacement motor boats will have a top speed of 5-12 knots depending upon their waterline length.

As an example, a generic displacement motor boat will have a maximum hull speed as follows:

Waterline length	Max hull speed
5m (16.4ft)	5.4 knots
10m (32.8ft)	7.7 knots
15m (49ft)	9.4 knots
20m (65.6ft)	10.9 knots
25m (82ft)	12.1 knots

So, for example, if you are contemplating the purchase of a 10m (32.8ft) displacement motor cruiser whose loving owner claims that she has a top speed of 10 knots, this should be treated with some suspicion unless she has sufficient power to move into the semi-displacement category. If in doubt, ask for a sea trial and see for yourself. If you wish to spend your time on canals or rivers then you should look for a displacement boat with naturally aspirated engines (no turbos). Turbos will be wasted on canals or rivers as speed limits will preclude the engines ever requiring their use.

Semi-displacement

If the optimum displacement power in a vessel is increased, the extra thrust produced will eventually cause the hull to start to rise out of the water and gain speed. Technically it will not plane, but its speed will increase beyond maximum displacement speed. This is known as semi-displacement. The best known semi-displacement motor cruisers are the round bilge 'Nelson' style launches, often used as pilot boats because of their extraordinary sea keeping characteristics, and the higher powered versions of American style trawler yachts such as Grand Banks and Traders. A large proportion of the extra power required to get them into the semi-displacement mode is used in throwing huge quantities of water aside as they force their way through the water. You can often recognise a semi-displacement motor boat from its huge bow wave long before you actually see the boat itself. Generally, semi-displacement motor boats will have a top speed of 12 -23 knots.

In a semi-displacement craft, engine power has been increased to exceed its maximum displacement speed to give 'lift' without actually planing. The term generally refers to the heavier, more traditional, seakindly boats such as this 'Nelson' style motor cruiser.

Semi-displacement craft include the American-style trawler yachts such as this 36ft Grand Banks Classic.

Above: Planing craft are built for speed: this SeaRay is capable of achieving 30 knots.
Left: Comparison of hull types.

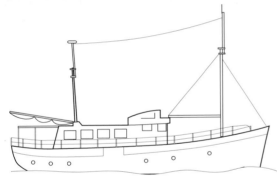

Displacement hull

Semi-displacement hull

Planing hull

Planing

In order to get the most efficient speed from a motor boat, it needs to plane. Once it gathers sufficient speed it will rise up out of the water and skim along on the surface achieving the least drag. The hull shape which achieves this the most efficiently is the Vee-shaped hull. Designers have spent many years trying to perfect the optimum relationship between the depth of the 'Vee' and the waterline length and the beam. Generally, the deeper the Vee, the softer the ride. The Vee will be deepest about one third of the way aft, but the angle (or deadrise as it is often called) is usually measured at the stern. The deadrise is likely to be between 10° and 23° at the stern. The larger the deadrise, the softer the ride and the better the hull will grip the water in a tight turn. There is, technically, no top limit to the speed of a planing hull but in realistic cruising terms it is likely to range between 13-45 knots. You may encounter 'stepped hulls'. These were originally designed for high speed racing craft. The 'steps' break the suction between the water and the hull thus reducing drag. Manufacturers claim that a stepped hull increases hull efficiency by around 10 per cent. Only time will tell as to whether stepped hulls become the norm for planing craft.

Engines

Single outboard

Probably the most simple means of propulsion is the single outboard. It may be started manually by pulling a starting cord or by an electric starter motor. The latter requires a battery which the engine will recharge once it starts running.

Outboards generally either run on petrol alone (four-stroke) or a mixture of petrol and oil (two-stroke). Some models run on diesel but this is unusual as diesel outboards are very bulky for their power output. Four-stroke petrol outboards will run surprisingly quietly and efficiently; two-stroke engines will give a better performance but use considerably more fuel. For servicing and general maintenance, outboards can be removed if necessary without too much trouble. Smaller models are attached to the transom (flat stern panel) of the boat with thumb screws and larger models are secured with through-transom bolts.

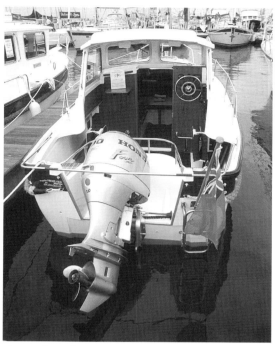

An outboard engine is commonly used to power smaller motor cruisers. Here the four-stroke on this Hardy Pilot is tilted to prevent the build up of marine growth when not in use.

Twin outboards

From a safety point of view, you would think that there is less chance of being caught out by an engine failure if you have two outboards to call upon. However engine failure is often caused by contaminated fuel so, if both engines run off the same tank, any advantage is lost. There is no great boat handling advantage of having twin outboards rather than just one. This is quite different from the advantage of twin shafts over a single shaft (see p 8).

Outdrives

Outdrives are a cross between an inboard engine and an outboard. Sometimes they are referred to as 'inboard/outboards', Z drives or 'legs'. In effect they enable a much larger engine to drive the propeller than would be possible with a

Outboard safety

Don't forget to lock the outboard onto your boat if you leave it unattended otherwise your insurance will not be valid. If you regularly remove the outboard, always ensure that you use a safety line. It is amazingly easy to allow an outboard to slip overboard whilst removing it. I know, I've done it.

Outdrives are often fitted on sports boats where greater power is needed than can be supplied by a conventional outboard. Left: the 'leg' is tilted up for launch and recovery and lowered for use. Right: the engine of an outdrive with the cover hinged forward.

conventional outboard. The propeller is situated behind the back of the boat on an outdrive leg which can be adjusted in and out (called power trim) to create the optimum propulsion angle to obtain the most comfortable ride and/or fastest speed. Outdrives are common on sports boats and motor cruisers up to about 11.5m (38ft). The larger boats with outdrives are difficult to control in strong winds when a bow thruster changes from being a luxury to a necessity. Some performance cruisers are fitted with three engines and outdrives for greater power and top performance.

Single shaft

One engine driving one shaft through the hull to one propeller is the conventional means of propulsion for vessels of all sizes. Anything from a slipper launch to a super tanker could be driven by this configuration. Boat handling requires some thought and single shafts are not usually sufficient to power planing craft. (There are exceptions such as the Nimbus range of 7.6-9m (25-30ft) cruisers which are single screw and have cruising speeds up to 24 knots.)

Twin shafts

Twin shafts are probably the commonest means of propulsion on motor cruisers

above 10.6m (35ft). Twin outward turning propellers make boat handling a delight once you get to grips with the technique and they obviate the need for a bow thruster; although if you are lucky enough to have both, there is really not much excuse for getting it wrong. An experienced helmsman can drive a twin screw motor boat into most tight spots without giving himself, or others, white knuckles.

Bow thrusters

Although not strictly a true source of propulsion, bow thrusters are becoming more and more popular and should be taken seriously as they can sometimes make the difference between a beautiful manoeuvre alongside and what is known in the trade as 'a heavy berthing'. Generally they consist of a propeller supported in a transverse tube through the hull in the bow of the vessel and, using either electrical or hydraulic power, they thrust water from one side to the other causing the bow of the boat to move sideways. They are not terribly efficient whilst the boat is making way (going along), but once she slows down to walking pace or less, the effect whilst tying up can be very helpful indeed. Some

Fuel consumption

Horse power	Diesel (per engine)		Two-stroke petrol (per engine)	
	Litres per hour	Imperial gallons per hour	Litres per hour	Imperial gallons per hour
25	5	1	9	2
50	11	2	17	4
75	17	3	26	6
100	23	5	34	7
150	35	8	51	11
200	46	10	68	15
300	69	15	102	22
500	115	25		
750	173	38	*These are approximate figures*	
1000	230	51	*for guidance only*	
1250	288	63		

single screw owners have discovered that they can be equally useful for steering the boat when moving slowly astern (backwards).

Fuel consumption

It is difficult to work out precisely how much fuel a boat will use but the table above will give a rough guide as to running costs.

Remember if you have more than one engine, you will need to double (or treble for three engines) the consumption. Four-stroke and OptiMax petrol outboards are generally 25-40 per cent more economical than their two-stroke equivalents.

It is difficult to compare miles per gallon in table format but an approximate guide is given below.

When you consider that marine diesel is around 20p–30p per litre, £1.00–£1.35 per imperial gallon (2000) and petrol at marinas is anything from 85p to £1.00 per litre, £3.86–£4.55 per imperial gallon (2000), fuel is a big consideration when buying a motor cruiser.

MPG guide

	Approx nautical miles per imperial gallon
• A single outboard RIB at 30 knots	5.00
• A single screw 9.5m (31ft) Nimbus at 16 knots	3.50
• A single screw river cruiser at 5 knots	3.00
• A single screw cruiser at 8 knots	2.00
• A twin screw 12m (39ft) Sealine at 20 knots	1.25
• A twin screw 14m (46ft) semi-displacement 'Nelson' at 18 knots	1.00
• A twin screw 13m (43ft) Grand Banks at 15 knots	0.75
• A twin screw 15m (49ft) Sunseeker at 30 knots	0.70
• A twin screw 20m (65.6ft) Fairline at 27 knots	0.35
• A twin screw 22m (72ft) Princess at 29 knots	0.28

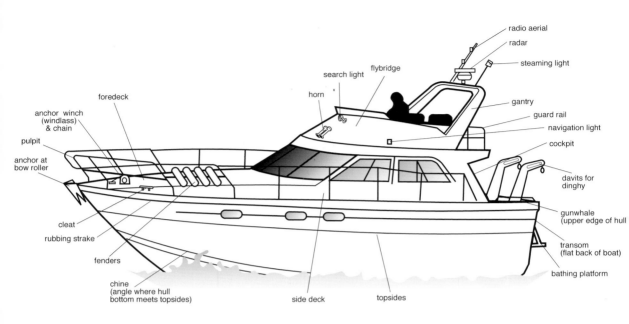

radio aerial
radar
steaming light
flybridge
search light
horn
foredeck
gantry
guard rail
anchor winch (windlass) & chain
navigation light
pulpit
cockpit
anchor at bow roller
davits for dinghy
cleat
gunwhale (upper edge of hull
rubbing strake
fenders
transom (flat back of boat)
bathing platform
chine (angle where hull bottom meets topsides)
side deck
topsides

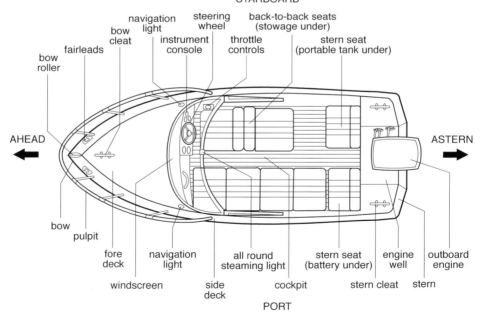

STARBOARD

navigation light
steering wheel
back-to-back seats (stowage under)
bow cleat
instrument console
throttle controls
stern seat (portable tank under)
fairleads
bow roller

AHEAD

ASTERN

bow pulpit

fore deck
navigation light
all round steaming light
stern seat (battery under)
engine well
outboard engine

windscreen
side deck
cockpit
stern cleat
stern

PORT

Deck layout of a typical motor cruiser.

How big a boat do you think you want?

I think it is true to say that everyone who has ever bought a boat has soon wished that they had bought the next size up! It's a bit like my experiences of buying computers. Always buy the size bigger than you think you need and you will rarely be disappointed. There are obviously limits to this, finance being probably the most restrictive. If you are thinking of towing your boat, look carefully at the towing limits imposed by the manufacturer of your car and remember that the weight limit imposed is the *total weight* including the boat, engine, trailer and all the gear and fuel which is in the boat whilst she is on the trailer. So a boat weighing 400kg (7.8cwt) might have a 150kg (3cwt) engine and a 200kg (4cwt) trailer. That's a total of 750kg (14.8cwt) without fuel, and all the other paraphernalia that you are likely to include for a day out. The police are taking a close interest in towing weights, as I discovered recently when pulled over and directed to a nearby weighbridge. I was amazed that although the boat, engine and trailer were in the brochure at 900kg (17.7cwt), the total weight I was towing including a full fuel tank, flares, lifejackets etc, totalled over 1100 kg (21.6cwt). Fortunately my car is capable of towing 1200kg (23.6cwt) but I was amazed how much closer I was to the limit than I had expected to be.

The Department of the Environment, Transport and the Regions regulations covering towing require trailers over 750kg maximum laden weight but under 3,500kg maximum laden weight to be fitted with an inertia braking system. Those under 750kg are not required to have such a system. Under no circumstances should the maximum laden weight of a trailer exceed the maximum permitted trailer weight recommended by a vehicle manufacturer.

Provided you remain within these restrictions no further driving licence is required. Ensure that your motor insurer is informed if you intend to tow.

Choose new or second-hand?

In my experience of boat buyers, there are three distinct categories: those who only buy new boats, those who only consider second-hand and a third group who are looking for a restoration project. The latter are a fascinating group. Their pleasure is in stripping and rebuilding old wrecks that have long since passed their sell-by date and restoring them to their former splendour. These owners probably have no intention of ever going to sea. Their enjoyment is in exercising their skill and money in restoring these 'old ladies'. Some restorations are better than others, so if you find yourself considering the purchase of a restoration project, always get a surveyor involved, as all may not be quite what it appears. Similarly, if you are considering embarking on a restoration project yourself, allow about five times as much time as you estimate and about ten times your initial budget if you really want to finish the job.

Where do you want to go boating?

Motor cruising is not really limited to any particular geographical area apart from the depth of the water in relation to the draught of your boat (ie the amount of water it needs to stay afloat) and proximity of places to visit which can keep you topped up with fuel. The availability of fuel is of vital importance to the motor cruiser owner and there are places in the country where petrol, for example, is very difficult

The slow-moving pace of inland waterway cruising suits many motorboaters who seek relaxing scenic trips with minimum stress.

to obtain; the stringent regulations controlling its storage have put many boatyards off the idea of supplying petrol. Diesel is generally less of a problem and, in the UK, it is a great deal cheaper than petrol because of differing rates of taxation on each product.

Fresh water cruising

There are two cruising options. First there is what one might call 'fresh water' cruising which is perhaps more realistically described as inland waterway cruising. Your progress is restricted to a gentle

potter by locally set speed limits, most of which are not much more than walking pace. These are policed vigorously so if you are contemplating using a boat on inland waterways, there is little point in buying a water dragster, as the opportunities for running it at much more than tick-over will be very severely restricted and closely monitored by the authorities.

Cruising through the canals of Britain or Europe can be a totally soothing and restful experience. The beauty of slowly changing scenery combined with multiple

If you intend to spend most of your holidays on your boat, you may find that it is a relatively economical option to keep her in a Mediterranean marina with the added bonus of fine weather cruising.

opportunities for short stops or a longer rest make for a very relaxing time indeed. No need to worry too much about how rough the canal is, how strong the tidal stream is, or whether or not going aground is a possibility.

Salt water cruising

The second option is 'salt water' cruising. This offers a very much more extensive cruising ground, but at the same time requires a more detailed knowledge of weather, tidal streams and general navigation. It is without doubt more interesting and varied as there are fewer geographical constraints. However it is very much more demanding and requires rather more of the boat owner in terms of expertise.

Many motor boat owners start off with a small river cruiser and once they have mastered boat handling and mooring skills, they move up to a larger cruiser and

venture further afield, having perhaps spent the winter months on an RYA shorebased training evening course. Further details of the RYA Training Scheme shorebased and practical courses are included in Appendix 8 on page 89.

So having decided on coastal cruising the next thing is to find an economical berth which is an easy drive from home if you want to visit your boat most weekends. If you live in the centre of the country you will probably have to resign yourself to long car journeys or opt for river and canal cruising instead.

There is a tremendous interest in motor cruising all along the south coast of England; the Solent area (between the mainland and the Isle of Wight) has the greatest density of pleasure boats in the whole of Europe. Needless to say it is also the most expensive place to keep a boat. What it does have, though, is plenty of sheltered water, interesting creeks and harbours to visit and it is only 60 miles from France which has a similarly fascinating coastline to explore.

As you move around the UK, there are marinas and harbours virtually all the way around the western side of the UK with really beautiful cruising grounds off north Wales and the western islands of Scotland where it can be idyllic when the weather is fair, but desperate when the weather turns foul. Nevertheless, it is still a very popular area for cruising.

The north-east coast tends to be rather commercial with big ferry and container ports and fishing harbours with little to attract motor cruisers.

The rather shallow and muddy East Anglian coastline has many fascinating unspoilt harbours which are well worth a visit but, because of the shallow nature of the coast, they tend to be frequented by sailing boats which take the bottom with rather better grace than motor cruisers.

The more adventurous may consider keeping a boat in the Mediterranean, attracted by the warm, if not hot, climate. You may worry about security whilst you are at home in the UK but it is usually possible to engage the services of a reliable *marinero* to keep an eye on your investment whilst you are away and to keep it clean. You will find that the Sahara Desert has the knack of whipping up strong southerly winds which very efficiently dump huge quantities of red muddy sand all over sparkling white motor cruisers from Gibraltar, along the Costa del Sol and out to the Balearics; if it is not washed off on a regular basis, it can turn into a horrible brown porridge blocking up deck drains and causing unnecessary grief.

Alternatively, you may dream of a base in the Caribbean. Again, you will need someone you can rely upon to keep an eye on your pride and joy when you are not there to do it yourself.

Creature comforts

Perhaps the largest culture shock to the new boat owning family or partnership is the close proximity in which you will find yourself living if you intend to venture out for more than day outings. It actually takes real skill and patience to live comfortably with others in a boat. Lots of fresh air and a completely new environment will inevitably be tiring. Assuming you have found a quiet, secure mooring, the gentle lapping of water on the hull and occasional rocking as other boats pass close by is very restful to most of us, and particularly to small children.

When contemplating your first purchase you should give a fair amount of thought to who is going to be regularly on board with you and what their needs will be:

- Do you have small children? If so, will they be able to move about the boat easily; are there enough safety features?
- Is the accommodation sufficient? Below deck layouts vary considerably and, as you may know from chartering experience, a four berth cruiser can be comfortable for two adults, reasonable for two adults and two small children but may be a definite squeeze for four adults.
- Try to visualise what it would be like for you and your family and/or friends to be *living* on the boat for a week. Will there be enough space? (See also page 31.)

The galley

Part of the fun of boating holidays is eating on board; a meal that might be considered a bit ordinary at home suddenly takes on a new perspective when served in a plastic dish on your lap in the cockpit of a gently bobbing motor cruiser.

So the galley is an area that needs consideration. It should be practical enough for your needs. Do you intend to use the boat just for weekends? If so you can probably manage with a two-burner cooker with grill, a work surface, a plastic bowl for washing up and a portable cold box. If, however, you plan longer holidays then a properly planned galley is important. It should be sited in a suitable position out of the way of the main traffic. Does the sink have a draining board? Is there adequate ventilation and reasonable storage and work space? Remember that a happy cook makes a happy ship.

Water supply

Water is one of the most important live-aboard considerations. No boat ever carries enough water. We all need to drink about eight glasses of water per day, it is said, to survive. Then we want to wash or shower and do some cooking and washing up and generally keep the boat clean. Before you know where you are, it is easy to use 40-50 litres (9-11 gallons) of water per person per day on a boat and think that you are being really abstemious. That adds up to a huge quantity for a small boat to carry. Even large charter yachts have problems supplying sufficient water for their guests and have to resort to making their own by using very expensive reverse osmosis plants. Just to put all this into perspective, when you are at home you will probably use or waste about 200 litres (44 gallons) every day. Therefore the water capacity needs to be adequate for your style of cruising. Most marinas offer water and many have showers and washing machines, so your cruising limitations are not solely constrained by your own water supply. But, nevertheless, it is a very important aspect to bear in mind when looking for a boat if you intend to live on board.

The heads

You may find the toilet arrangements or 'heads' rather 'quaint' to say the least. Boat showers and wash basins are prone to blockages of surplus hair and other detritus but the intricacies of a manually-operated toilet leave most newcomers gasping for inspiration. You will need to pin up a strict set of dos and don'ts for visitors to avoid trouble. Only last season I was cruising around the Balearics and one of my passengers managed to block up the entire plumbing system and, as skipper, I was saddled with the unsavoury task of sorting it out.

It is possible that the boat you are considering comes complete with a chemical toilet. The 'porta potti' concept also takes a bit of coming to terms with. Generally they are found in smaller sports boats and come as a complete self-contained unit which slides out of sight under steps or seats when not in use. Before use, it is necessary to pull it out, usually in the centre of the cabin which is not to everybody's liking. You also have to remember to keep emptying the sullage and maintain it topped up with chemical fluid.

Who's going to be your crew?

So far I have assumed that your boating activities are restricted to a family affair. That is by no means the only alternative. There are a few single-handed motor cruiser owners around but it is not a practice that is encouraged just in case a serious mishap occurs when the presence of an extra crew member can be vital.

You may have friends who are not in the financial position to be boat owners themselves but have gained experience in other boats and are keen to join you. Wherever your crew comes from, make an effort to get to know their strengths and weaknesses so that, in the unlikely event of disaster striking, you know who you can count upon to do what.

15

What's it really like out there amongst the serpents and the dragons?

You don't tend to see too many serpents or dragons on the inland waterways, but if you are considering venturing out of sight of land, it would be prudent to do so with someone who has previous boathandling experience. The first time that the shoreline disappears over the horizon is one of those moments that you will never forget. For some people it is very disorientating. Make sure you have a steering compass and that it has been adjusted after it was fitted in the boat. If you ignore this advice, be aware that it is quite possible, indeed normal, for a steering compass to read as much as 60° out on some courses but not necessarily the same on others. The fact that the boat may be new has no bearing on this. You have been warned.

Make sure you have a weather forecast with you and that you understand what it means. As a rule of thumb, if the forecast indicates light winds from force 1-3, everything should be fine. If it creeps up the Beaufort Scale to force 4 or 5, and you are in any doubt, then stay tied up. Once it gets to force 6 or over, definitely stay at home. The marine forecasts given by local Met Offices and coastguards are generally highly reliable. If you think that the forecast may be wrong, it is most likely that it is the *timing* and *not the impending weather* that is incorrect. So if you hear a gale warning and you can't see any sign of it, you can be assured it will certainly be out there somewhere.

The sea is most definitely a force to be reckoned with and you should only venture out when you are confident of what you, your boat and your crew can cope with. The Bay of Biscay can, in my experience, be the most beautiful cruising ground with its enormous, long, gentle swell – if you get the forecast right. Equally it can be a real nightmare if you get caught out, as I did in October 1987 when the unexpected and now notorious hurricane came through. The size and ferocity of the sea combined with the screaming wind was totally unbelievable and, without doubt, one of those moments I shall never forget. The one thing to remember is that a well-found and well maintained boat will take far more abuse from bad weather than the average sailor. So just because *you* may have had enough, you can generally be assured that your boat will still have an in-built determination to get you safely home. You must never forget that, especially when you are down on your knees with your hands together and it seems that all may be lost.

2

Buying a New Boat

First a few words of caution: those people who order a brand new boat expecting it to be delivered on time, perfect in every detail and ready to drive away are, in my experience, generally disappointed. However, if you are happy to put up with the initial teething problems of owning a new boat, then you have the advantages of being able to specify the equipment, colour scheme and, perhaps most importantly, the name of your new baby. I mention the name at this point because if you have not owned a boat before, you should know that it is considered bad luck for a boat to change its name during its life.

Where do you begin to look?

Boating magazines are jammed full of glossy adverts and detailed tests of new models, but you should bear in mind that boat test writers are constrained to some extent by their magazine's editorial and advertising policy. Nevertheless once you

Southampton Boat Show is the ideal venue to look at the range of new boats on offer – many are actually afloat and some available for demonstrations. The lively atmosphere at the show also makes it a very enjoyable day out for the family.

have read one or two, you will soon get a feel for the writer's drift even though the words themselves may be a little on the enthusiastic side. Boat shows are the best place to see the widest range of new boats. There you will see a vast selection either ashore or afloat, according to the location of the show, and get a feel for the market and the type of boat which will fit into your budget and aspirations. Generally, the two or three weekends following a boat show are used by dealers for sea trials so serious buyers can go along and see the boat in action before parting with any money.

EU Recreational Craft Directive

To help you in your deliberations of how suitable a boat is, the European Union (EU) initiated a Recreational Craft Directive (RCD) on 16 June 1998 introducing minimum standards to which new boats built within the EU, or imported into it, have to conform. Pleasure boats with a hull length of more than 2.5m (8.2ft) but less than 24m (78.7ft) are divided into four categories of sea-going suitability (see box below).

This gives a yardstick against which you can measure the suitability of a new craft against your own requirements. Obviously it can only give you a guide and remember that these are minimum standards, but if you are considering two seemingly similar vessels but each having different RCD categories, it will help you to compile a series of questions to put to manufacturers

to lead you towards the boat which really should fulfil your needs.

Buyer beware

You might think that buying a new boat would be much simpler than buying a second-hand one. Well, let me tell you that if you are a first time buyer, you are the new boat salesman's dream. He can promise you the world and you are unlikely to know any different. If there are particular requirements which you have, then they must be in writing so that there is no doubt in anyone's mind as to what you are expecting. If you need to do a minimum of 25 knots, this should be part of the agreement. If you need a range of 200 miles, make this clear. Incidentally, it is usual to calculate range leaving a reserve of 20 per cent of fuel in the tank. So if you need a usable range of 200 miles, ask for a minimum range of 250 miles. If time is of the essence and you need the boat to be delivered by a particular date, insist that it is included in the contract and there should be a penalty clause for late delivery. Few boats in my experience are ready when the purchaser expects and recently I have just been involved with the purchase of a new boat which was six months late.

Unfortunately, the inexperienced first time buyer provides the ideal opportunity for the less scrupulous boat builder to offload all the old fittings and equipment which have been rejected by previous customers and are gathering dust in his store. You may not realise the significance of the subtle changes to the specification

Category	Suitability	Mean wave heights
A	Ocean	More than 4 metres (13ft 1in)
B	Offshore	Up to 4 metres (13ft 1in)
C	Inshore	Up to 2 metres (6ft 7in)
D	Sheltered Waters	Up to 0.5 metres (1ft 8in)

One of the attractions of buying a new boat is the delight of stepping into a gleaming, pristine interior though the price of this luxury 22 metre Princess will be the equivalent to that of a period country cottage.

during the progress of the build and be perfectly happy until you invite a knowledgeable friend aboard who asks why you chose this, this or this? As a first time buyer you are very vulnerable. It is therefore well worth considering appointing a surveyor to oversee the construction of your boat from the initial hull moulding through to the sea trials. The boat builder will positively discourage this and point out that he has built huge quantities of this particular model and that a surveyor is really not necessary. To any boat builder, as you can probably imagine, independent surveyors are a potential hindrance which they could well do without. You have to weigh up the cost of appointing a surveyor against the possibility of not necessarily getting the latest state-of-the-art boat which you were expecting. Naturally, not all boat builders are like this, but I have seen it happen on

more than a few occasions, so do keep your wits about you as a first time buyer.

The contract

Once you get to the stage where your hand is itching to sign the cheque, you need to get clear in your own mind with whom you are dealing and whether this person or firm is in fact the builder of the boat, the builder's dealer or an agent acting on behalf of the builder or dealer. The Sale of Goods Act 1979 designates responsibility for servicing the warranty to the person, firm or company with whom you have made the contract. Therefore, if you buy a boat from the agent of a boat builder, it is the agent who should carry out any warranty work. The practicalities of this from a geographical viewpoint need to be recognised. If the agent is based in

Scotland but you plan to keep the boat in the south of England, you may have a problem in getting much satisfaction. Many dealers and agents have offices all over the world to cope with this situation but it is best to check this out early.

No matter how legal, decent, honest and truthful the salesman looks, you would be ill advised to part with any money until a formal contract for the purchase is established. You, as the purchaser, will have very different expectations from the builder, dealer or agent. You are likely to be asked to make stage payments on all but the smallest new boats. This is a quite normal requirement but you do need to be cautious.

The greatest potential disaster is the builder becoming insolvent before or during the construction of the boat. In particular you should beware of putting down a deposit of more than 5 per cent or 10 per cent, and certainly be very cautious about special boat show offers requiring you to put down more than 10 per cent. On a number of occasions in recent years the flow of extra money into an insolvent company after a boat show has prompted the builder's bank to put the company into receivership, and unfortunate buyers have lost their deposits. There is a standard form of agreement issued by the British Marine Industries Federation (BMIF) and approved by the RYA (see Appendix 3) which, as far as possible, equitably satisfies the reasonable requirements of both builder and purchaser. However, it is important that you read the small print very carefully and, if in any doubt whatsoever, take professional advice.

Stage payments

The amount most at risk in the purchase of a new boat is the initial deposit. At the time you hand it over, there is unlikely to be anything of tangible value relating to the new boat in existence against which

you can claim, so it is inadvisable to pay more initially than is absolutely necessary. Generally, you will be asked for between 10 and 25 per cent up front. Looking at it pessimistically, don't hand over a greater deposit than, in the worst possible scenario, you can afford to lose. If you find yourself in this unhappy situation, the receiver's first task in unravelling the problem will be to read the contracts relating to part-built boats very carefully to establish who owns what. It is in your interests therefore to ensure that each payment which you make is attributed to the construction of your boat and the contract should include a paragraph stating that the materials acquired or appropriated for the construction of the boat shall become the property of the purchaser upon the payment of the first instalment but at the same time, in order to give the builder similar comfort, that the builder shall have a lien (right to hold the property until debts are paid) on the craft, materials and equipment for all sums due. That way you, as purchaser, maintain a financial interest in the boat whilst under construction. A practical way to demonstrate this is for each component delivered to the builder to be immediately marked with your boat's name or build reference number and in fact this is a requirement of the BMIF standard form agreement.

Another alternative would be to seek a bank guarantee that in the event of the builder being unable to complete the construction, any monies paid will be returned. Frankly, the likelihood of being offered one of these in most cases equates only to the likelihood of flying pigs. A small builder might be persuaded to give a personal guarantee against failure to complete a construction but realistically, even if you were to make a successful claim, in practical terms you are totally reliant upon his personal ability and not

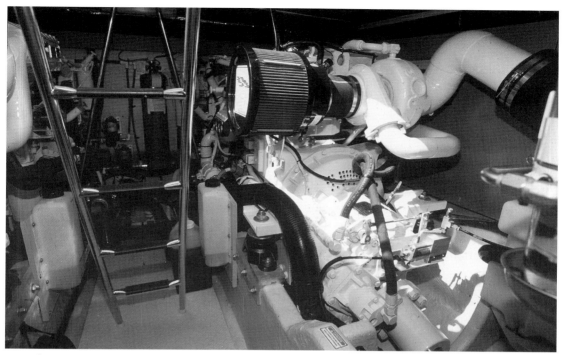

An advantage to buying a new boat is that it has no history and the engine is at the beginning of its working life.

his personal willingness to repay. In practical terms, why not ask for a financial report of the trading position of the company which your bank or accountant or a quick surf on the Internet can provide for a limited company. This will not offer you any guarantees but it may give you some peace of mind.

The type of contract that you should be very wary of is one which demands a deposit or stage payments but does not pass ownership of the boat to the purchaser until the whole sale price has been paid.

If you require the boat to be delivered fully operational for a particular date, you may choose to insist that a late delivery clause is added to the contract. You certainly won't be offered this as standard for obvious reasons but it would not be unreasonable to ask for penalty payments of a fixed amount per day in the event of

the boat being delivered late without reasonable cause.

Having mentioned how important it is that you establish some legal title to your part-built boat, you should also make sure that your interests are insured against building risks. This can be done in one of two ways, either by having your interest noted on the builder's insurance policy or, better still, by taking out your own boat construction risks cover for the duration of the build.

Safeguards

Until recently there were no wide-reaching safeguards in the boat building trade ensuring that boats were built to a particular standard. Indeed even now, a certificate from Lloyd's or other Certification Society is given based upon the general design and standard of build of the class and not of individual vessels. The

CE marking indicates a Category which has been assigned based upon information taken from the design and construction methods used. Neither are independently checked against every individual vessel so I am a great believer in appointing your own surveyor – if not to oversee the whole build, then certainly to inspect the boat when she is completed and to witness her sea trials before you make the last payment. Sea trials are an important aspect of buying a new boat and you would be well advised to ensure that the contract includes the opportunity to see the boat in action before you hand over the last few pounds. It would not be unreasonable to include in the contract that the buyer should withhold the final 5-10 per cent of the purchase price until the sea trials are satisfactorily completed. You need to remember that the final payment is probably the only one which actually includes any profit margin for the builder, so he will be very keen to receive it at the earliest opportunity.

VAT

The European Union (EU) decreed in early 1993 that Value Added Tax (or its equivalent) had to be paid on all boats built or imported into the EU. Initially this caused a number of difficulties for owners in proving the VAT status of their boat but fortunately most of these problems have now passed and the VAT status of boats is generally clear. A new boat built or imported into the EU requires that VAT should be paid. There are one or two exceptions, of which most details are available in Chapter 10 and Appendix 5, but you can be sure that as time goes on, the determination of the EU to stop tax avoidance is likely to increase. At present, if you decide to keep your boat in a country outside the EU or in Dependencies which are outside the EU tax area, you can still do so without paying VAT but for how long that will be the case, only time will tell. You need to remember that if you subsequently wish to use the boat in the EU or sell the boat to someone who wants to keep her in the EU that VAT will have to be paid on the boat's value at the point of sale. This therefore will affect the sale proceeds. Specialist marine lawyers or the RYA legal team will be able to give an update on the situation on a day-to-day basis. The importance of knowing your boat's tax status and being able to prove it will become apparent if you decide to venture across the Channel or North Sea. Customs officers on the other side are likely to peruse your boat's VAT status with great interest. Like every other possession of an EU citizen, freedom of movement is only allowed of VAT-paid status goods. The difference is that, with boats, this VAT status sometimes needs to be proved.

3

Buying a Second-hand Boat

Having mentioned the frustrations of buying new, it is pretty obvious that buying second-hand opens a much larger range of potential disasters. However, if you take care in the selection of your second-hand boat, unexpected surprises should be kept to a minimum. Obviously you are likely to pay less for a second-hand boat than a new one but you will not have the choice of the specification or colour scheme. If you are even slightly superstitious you won't want to change the name. The moral of the story is if you don't like the equipment, colour or name then don't buy it. There are always plenty more available. Another fact you should know about boats is that, unlike most things in life, every boat is 'for sale' from the day she is launched until the day she ends up in the place where old boats go. So if you find your dream boat, and discover that she is not actually being advertised for sale, no owner is going to be offended if you make an approach with a view to buying her. They can only say 'No'. Even my father's most beautiful pre-war motor yacht, which he had loved and cherished for almost 30 years, was sold to a very determined purchaser rather than an inclination on Dad's part to sell. In fact I never thought that he would ever part with her. I guess the price *was* right.

Many more people buy second-hand boats than new and there are several advantages. A second-hand craft will inevitably cost less than her new equivalent. She will almost certainly be fitted with more equipment than is

standard and the initial niggles and leaks that are part of the joys of buying a new boat will, hopefully, have been ironed out. If she has been regularly and carefully used and maintained, a second-hand boat should be a good buy. The important things to watch out for are that:

- The boat is free from any major defects.
- She actually belongs to the seller.
- There are no outstanding debts, bills or mortgages against the boat including VAT payment.

Finding your boat

One of the best starting points is to look in the boating magazines – most have classified adverts and by studying these you can get an idea of the market and comparative prices. A selection of useful titles is listed in Appendix 9. There are even some dedicated 'boats for sale' magazines with a countrywide range of different craft on offer. If you live near the coast and are looking for a modestly priced cruiser, you may find what you are looking for in the local 'free ad' papers or chandlers' notice boards. Once you have spotted an interesting advert write out a checklist of essential information and have a good chat with the seller – he or she will probably be quite forthcoming if you ask the right questions and this may save you making an unnecessary lengthy journey to view an unsuitable boat; ask if they have a typed specification or any pictures of the boat which they can send to you,

If you take a stroll round any large marina you will frequently see boats advertised for sale by their owners. If you chat to boatowners on the pontoons you may learn about other boats which may be available.

especially if the boat is located a long way from your home. Once you have found something suitable to look at, try to take a knowledgeable friend, whose judgement you trust, along with you so you can compare opinions afterwards. Take some notes and photos if possible; it is amazing how hazy your memory of layout and equipment details will be by the time you have driven home. View as many boats as possible because the more knowledge you have, the better your final choice will be.

Boatyards can be good hunting grounds for second-hand boats. If the boat is laid up you then have the advantage of being able to have a good look at her hull and propellers (see Chapter 5) but if you are really keen to buy you should ask to see her in the water so that you can judge the performance of the engine(s) and check her handling. The owner may be reluctant

to arrange this as it will be costly to have her floated but you could make it a condition of sale that you or your representative (this could be your surveyor) take the boat out on a sea trial before the deal is closed.

It is quite likely that you will find a boat through a broker or agent most of whom will belong to the British Marine Industry Federation (BMIF) or the Association of Brokers and Yacht Agents (ABYA). By their membership, they will support and promote the British Industry Code of Practice for the Sale of Used Boats. This lays down the guidelines which safeguard the purchaser as well as the seller and ensure fair play for those involved. It is sensible to check with the broker or agent whether their business is conducted in accordance with the Code of Practice. If it is not, and there are some very reputable

When buying a second-hand boat you will inevitably get plenty of equipment, particularly navigation aids, either included in the sale or negotiable at a reasonable price.

agents and brokers who for one reason or another choose not to follow the Code but to conduct their business in a different but equally acceptable way, you would be advised to scrutinise their contract more closely.

The negotiations

If you really start to get interested you suddenly find yourself sucked into negotiations. You will either relish it or hate it. If nothing gets your adrenaline going better than a good old-fashioned face-to-face hard-nosed session with the seller, then boat buying will be right up your street. However, if you are a first time buyer, you will need to do a lot of homework about boats before you get a feel of what you might expect to be

included in the purchase and what owners expect to keep. In the main, you want included in the sale all the peripheral equipment you can. If the dinghy, liferaft, fenders, ropes, flares, bedding etc are included in the deal, you could save thousands. If the boat is stripped down to the barest minimum, be aware that you will need to purchase certain equipment before setting off for the first time. If useful equipment is available for separate negotiations, this gives you an opportunity to make an offer subject to all the extras being included.

Moorings are another point of discussion. Can you continue to use the existing mooring until the end of the season? It will almost certainly have already been paid for if you are buying after April; however, some moorings are transferable and some are not.

Always enter negotiations with an alternative boat up your sleeve which you are also supposedly considering which has more to offer at a similar price. Keep the vendor on his toes. He will be far more keen to sell the boat than you imagine. The things that will encourage him are your ability to complete the deal quickly and with minimum formality. So if you are thinking of a loan or marine mortgage, speak to the lenders early and get an agreement in principle to lend you the amount you anticipate.

Unlike buying a house in England where we seem to enjoy remaining on tenterhooks until the contracts have been exchanged, a verbal contract to buy a boat is binding from the moment you agree the price, and the price becomes payable within a reasonable time. It is sensible therefore to consider one or two provisos with your offer. For example '*I am prepared to offer £XXXXX for your boat subject to a satisfactory sea trial and a survey*'. This is then quite clear to both parties and, in order to show your positive intention, it would be usual to pay a deposit of up to 10 per cent. Once the deposit has been paid you will then need to appoint a marine surveyor and engineer and arrange for a sea trial. (See Chapter 4.)

Proof of title

If you find yourself in the position of dealing direct with the seller, then you need to be sure that the proof of title given by the seller is watertight. If the boat is registered on Part I of the Register of British Ships, you can contact them and, for a fee, they will confirm the name and address of the owner and whether there are any financial charges over the boat from third parties who may also have an interest in her. If the boat is registered on Part III (Small Ships Register (SSR)), you

will not have that comfort. The SSR gives the name and address of the keeper but this is not necessarily the owner in legal terms and they will have no record of charges over the vessel. Whatever the outcome you would be well advised to draw up a contract and Appendix 2 gives an example of a contract for the sale of a second-hand boat approved by the Royal Yachting Association.

VAT

The tax situation needs careful scrutiny. Has VAT or the equivalent in another EU country been paid on the boat? Has VAT been reclaimed? Has the boat changed hands outside the EU? Are you being offered proof of payment? If not, you need to be absolutely sure that you cannot get caught for it later. Chapter 10 and Appendix 5 both give details on VAT.

The purchase

Once you are satisfied that the boat is what you were expecting and any niggles and defects have been ironed out or the price adjusted accordingly, you can proceed with the purchase. Before parting with the balance though, be sure that you have a contract signed by both parties together with any existing registration documentation and that, if the boat is registered on Part I of the Registry, the seller is the current registered owner. If not you have the headache of sorting out Bills of Sale between the last registered owner and yourself and everyone who has owned the boat in between.

If the boat is registered on Part III of the Registry, changing the name of the owner is much less formal and sending the old registration card together with details of the new owner is all that is required.

4

Yacht Brokers & Surveyors – are They Really Necessary?

Buying through a broker

It is quite likely that your first entry into the boating market will be through a yacht broker. Adverts appear in all the boating magazines and a careful study of these over a few months will give you an idea as to the types of vessel available in your price range. Don't rush in! There are always plenty more boats for sale and if you make it obvious that you are a first time buyer (and you will find it difficult not to), you will quite likely be made to feel that if you don't decide immediately, you will miss out on the bargain of the century. I have spent a lifetime seriously searching for the bargain of the century so far without any real success.

One advantage of going to a broker is that he will probably be able to show you a choice of several boats which will help you to get a clear idea of the right one for your purpose. Although the broker acts as an agent for the owner, if he is a member of the Association of Brokers and Yacht Agents or the British Marine Industry Federation he will follow rules for transactions laid down by these governing bodies.

The difference between buying a boat and buying a house is that a solicitor inevitably gets involved when buying a house but few people engage a solicitor to oversee the purchase of a boat. You are therefore very much reliant on the yacht broker who is selling the boat to ensure that your purchase goes through without mishap. Fortunately the majority of yacht brokers are members of the ABYA (Association of Brokers and Yacht Agents) or the BMIF (British Marine Industry Federation), both being trade associations of some stature, which hopefully should enable you to sleep peacefully during your negotiations and whilst your deposit is being held.

If you are contemplating the purchase of a second-hand boat and all the signs look good, it is the usual practice to make an offer. (Make sure you are serious as a verbal offer to buy is legally binding.) Once you and the vendor have agreed a figure, you will be invited to put down a 10 per cent deposit.

Any offer you make should be subject to survey. Don't be tempted to think that just because it looks nice that there are no real nasties hiding undiscovered. The deposit will be held by the broker as stakeholder and he will act as the arbiter once the boat has been surveyed should anything unexpected come to light.

The surveyor

There is in fact no obligation to have a boat surveyed, but I strongly recommend that you appoint a surveyor to inspect the boat on your behalf. There are no yacht surveying qualifications as such, but most yacht surveyors will belong to a trade association such as the YDSA (Yacht Designers and Surveyors Association).

Perhaps the most important aspect to check is whether your chosen surveyor is protected by professional indemnity (PI) insurance. If so, you will have some comfort that he has credibility within yacht surveying circles and if he makes a complete botch of your survey, you will have some redress against him or his insurance company.

As your boat is powered by engines, you would be well advised to ensure that the surveyor you appoint is sufficiently experienced to pass a professional opinion on the mechanics as well as the structure, or if not that you employ an experienced marine engineer to accompany you on a sea trial to check the engine(s) running under load and to comment upon any claims made by the seller about performance or fuel consumption – it will be money well spent. Make sure that the engineer also has PI insurance. This will give some peace of mind that if an important defect is missed, you will have some recourse.

In order to have a structural survey completed, the boat will need to be lifted out of the water (at your own expense) and within a few days of the surveyor's visit, your report will arrive. Unless the surveyor or engineer has revealed a material defect with the boat which you could not possibly have foreseen, you will be committed to the purchase. However if there are problems which arise, which can be remedied at a reasonable cost, you have a choice of either withdrawing from the purchase or entering into negotiation to reduce the sale price by the amount it will cost to remedy these problems. If you are dealing through a broker, your deposit will be held by him as stakeholder and he will act as the negotiator between you and the seller but you should realise that a few little repairable niggles will not enable you to withdraw from the sale without losing your deposit. So don't part with a deposit unless you really want to buy the boat.

Fees

All this costs money but in the long run, it is money well spent. Unless the survey reveals a real floating disaster, it will serve as evidence to enable you to adjust your offer price to an amount which takes into account any work which may be required so you may more than recoup the cost of the survey in the end.

The following table will give an approximate idea as to the cost of a yacht survey carried out by a YDSA Member:

Size of boat	Survey fee
7.5m (25ft)	£230
10m (33ft)	£375
15m (50ft)	£800
20m (65ft)	£1500

Surveyors will always quote in advance for the cost of a survey report but don't forget to check whether VAT or any travelling expenses are included or need to be added.

As to whether they are really necessary, I have bought and sold boats for more than twenty years and whilst, on occasions, I have bought boats privately where a broker was not involved, I wouldn't dream of buying a boat without my long-standing surveyor having a look first. He doesn't usually find anything I've missed, but he has on odd occasions, and once he saved me a *serious* amount of money.

Legal rights

Under the Supply of Goods & Services Act 1982, professional contractors (this includes marine surveyors and engineers) are 'expected to exercise the degree of skill and care that all the circumstances of the case requires'. If you discover a defect that another surveyor subsequently advises should have been noted by the original surveyor, then you would have a claim against the first surveyor. This is why it is important to ensure that your chosen surveyor has professional indemnity insurance.

Section 14 of the Sale of Goods Act 1979 gives the buyer a right to expect that the goods are fit for purpose but only if the boat is being sold to you by someone in the course of his business. So if you choose to buy privately or from a broker, this protection does not exist. You do however have protection against being told a pack of lies under Section 13 whether the seller is selling in the course of his business or not. So if the owner or broker tells you facts about the boat which are subsequently proved to be rubbish, you would have reason to pursue the seller or broker through the courts. This, though, is much easier to write about than to achieve in practice as it will inevitably end up with one man's word against another.

5

What You Can See For Yourself

When the boat buying bug bites, you need to keep your wits about you. My advice is *never* go looking for a boat on your own. Always take someone along who knows about boats but has absolutely no interest whatsoever in whether you buy a boat or not. It is very easy for a first time buyer to be lured into seriously considering the most appalling heaps of rubbish.

The next thing which may surprise you is the dreadful state in which many people leave their boats. You may find washing up still in the sink, untidy bunks, and mould in the toilet or shower compartment. Unfortunately some owners either get bored with their investment or simply run out of money and just leave the boat to deteriorate. Unless the exterior is washed down regularly and the interior is kept well ventilated, viewing second-hand boats can be an eye and nose boggling adventure.

If you find that (even after the initial shock) the main framework of the boat still has some undeniable attraction for you, this is where you need to get your disinterested but knowledgeable companion involved. Ask for all the disadvantages to be pointed out. Be brave and listen. If you ignore objective advice at this stage, it may result in an unnecessarily expensive and wasteful day out. However, it could be that your first viewing turns out to be a really pleasurable experience. I hope it is.

The vendor

Good signs to look out for are as follows:
- The owner has used the boat regularly.
- He has spent time and effort in preparing it for sale.
- He has a credible reason for selling.
- His boat is not going to involve you in enormous additional cost or effort to make it seaworthy or suitable for your purpose.

The ideal vendor is one who has loved and cherished his investment for many years and has reached the age when retirement from boating has arrived. He will have no future use for all the gear on board and, providing you give him the impression that you will take care of his 'baby' in the same way that he has, you could well be on to a winner. Price will probably not be of the utmost importance; he will want to satisfy himself, though, that you will take good care of his boat.

The viewing checklist

As a first time buyer, it is very difficult to know where to begin. Do not worry too much about the general state of cleanliness or hygiene; these are easy problems to solve. Try to imagine how the boat is going to satisfy your aspirations. First ask yourself:

Believe it or not, this boat was actually for sale in this condition in a boatyard. Be wary of any boat with as much marine growth as this as it has obviously been moored up unattended for some time.

- Is she really the type of boat you planned to buy?
- Is the price within, or realistically close to, your budget?
- How much money will you need to spend on her?
- Does she have sufficient accommodation?
- Will her claimed speed performance match your expectations?
- Will her fuel capacity enable you to get far enough afield without needing to refill?
- Does the galley offer sufficient cooking facilities for your gastronomic aims and desires?
- Does she carry enough water? (You will probably find that the answer to this will inevitably be 'No' but you must consider just how far short she falls.)

The sleeping arrangements
- Are the bunks all 6ft 3in (1.90m) long or more?
- How tall are you and your family?
- How tall is that lanky son of yours likely to end up?
- Many boats are built with bunks which are barely 6ft (1.83m) long which anyone 5ft 9in (1.75m) or more tall will find really uncomfortable.
- Don't worry too much if the bunks seem rather narrow. Wide bunks are actually quite difficult to stay in if the boat is underway and she is rolling around.

The living accommodation
- Is there sufficient seating for anticipated crew and passengers when the boat is underway?
- Can they see out of the windows? No one will stay seated for long if they can't see where they're going.

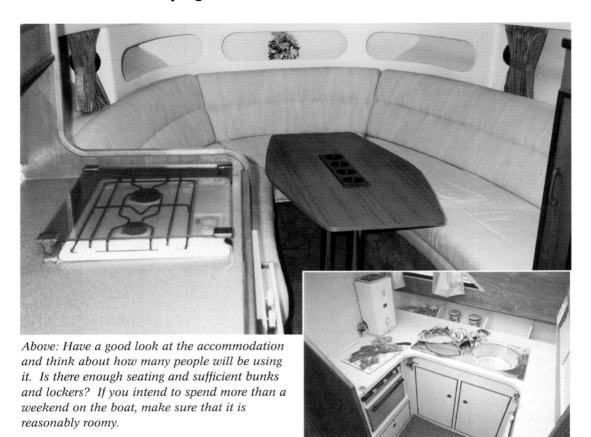

Above: Have a good look at the accommodation and think about how many people will be using it. Is there enough seating and sufficient bunks and lockers? If you intend to spend more than a weekend on the boat, make sure that it is reasonably roomy.

Right: Check the galley to see if it has all the basics you feel you need. This galley may be small but the designers have managed to fit in a double sink, water heater, cooker with oven and grill, a refrigerator plus lockers too (Photo: Broom Boats).

- Are there plenty of lockers?
- Does she have a decent range of electrical and electronic equipment?
- Does it work? Never assume that just because it is installed that it works.
- Is there gas for cooking? If so, is there a gas detector?
- Is the gas cylinder in a gas-tight compartment which drains overboard so that in the event of a gas leak, it doesn't settle in the bilge and become an explosive hazard? (Don't forget that propane is heavier than air.)
- What type of heater is installed? Is it safe for use with children? Is there adequate ventilation?

The galley

Perceived attributes of a galley depend on how much cooking you intend to do whilst cruising. If preparing food is not going to be your job, make sure that the cook gets a chance to assess the facilities.

- Is the galley in a good position?
- Is it easy and safe to use? Visualise preparing a meal for four people.
- Is there enough stowage space for food and cooking utensils?
- Do the lockers shut securely?
- Is there a sink? How is the water supplied and removed? Ask to see this.

The engine(s)

- Do they look freshly painted? If so, ask why.
- Are they covered with salt crystals, oily deposits or stains?
- Is the bilge area under the engine(s) (or drip tray(s)) full of oil, diesel or water?

None of these is a good sign.

Try opening and closing an engine cooling water sea suction seacock.

- Does it move easily?
- Has it been maintained?
- Could you close it in an emergency?

Pull out the dip stick(s) to see what colour the engine oil is. It will probably be dark brown or black unless it has been recently changed in which case it could be any shade from clear through yellow and light brown to dark brown or black. The oil should run down the dip stick easily. If it is thick like treacle, it suggests lack of maintenance. If there are signs of milkiness in the oil, it could indicate an internal water leak which could be expensive to cure.

- Are the drive belts worn?

Move aft to the gear box(es).

- Pull out the gear box dip stick.
- This oil should be absolutely clean and clear or it may be tinted pink or purplish if automatic transmission fluid has been used as, for example, in Borg Warner gearboxes.

If the boat is fitted with fuel filters which separate water from fuel into a glass bowl, have a look in the bowl for signs of water or debris. Black slime could indicate previous signs of a biological growth which degrades diesel and blocks filters and pipes. If there are any signs of jelly or strings of fine 'frog spawn' strands floating in the bowl, there is definitely a living biological growth in the tank. This can be overcome with the use of biocides

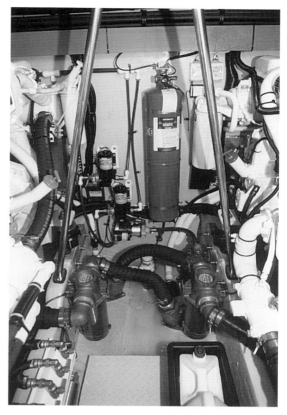

Check to see if there is a fire extinguisher in the engine compartment and that it is in date.

but it is an aggravation you could do without. This is most likely in boats which have not been used for a while. If you get as far as a sea trial on a boat which you know has had little use, take a look afterwards to see if any growths have been drawn through.

- Check if there is a fire extinguisher in the engine compartment. Is it in date?

The electrics

- Are there sufficient batteries?
- Are there separate batteries for both engine starting and domestic and navigation equipment?
- Are the batteries stored safely?
- Does the wiring look neat and tidy or is it a spaghetti-like tangle (possibly

Recommended safety equipment

- Anchor with warp and chain appropriate to size of cruiser
- Bucket
- Bilge pumps (hand and electric)
- Radar reflector
- Fixed navigation lights (with spare bulbs)
- Powerful waterproof torch
- Pyrotechnics: hand-held red flares; hand-held orange smoke signals; buoyant orange smoke signals; red parachute rockets; hand-held white flares. Note: if pyrotechnics are sold with the boat, check that they are in date and that you know how to use them.
- Fire fighting equipment. The galley should have a fire blanket and a 1.5kg dry powder extinguisher plus another for the engine compartment and the saloon. Check with your insurer as they may have certain minimum requirements.
- Personal safety equipment: warm clothing; lifejacket or buoyancy aid of approved type
- Liferaft or tender
- Horseshoe life belts fitted with drogue and self-igniting light

- Buoyant heaving line (30m (98ft) in length)
- Dan buoy
- VHF radio
- Charts of your intended cruising areas plus tide tables
- Steering compass
- Echo sounder
- Barometer
- Watch or clock
- First aid kit
- Warp suitable for towing
- Mooring warps and fenders
- Tool kit for engine
- Spares for engine: spare fuel filter, oil filter, water pump impeller, engine and gearbox oil, belts, fuses, light bulbs
- Emergency water supply separate from main tank
- Softwood plugs and wedges

Whilst this list is not comprehensive, it gives an idea of the things to look for on a second-hand boat which, if included in the sale, can save you quite a lot of outlay.

indicating an amateur electrician at work)? Bear in mind that rewiring costs may be expensive.

- Is there a generator? Does it work?
- Does the control panel look well laid out?

The heads

If the lavatorial arrangements include a sea toilet, try flushing it.

- If you don't know how, get the vendor to show you.
- Does water pump in and then flush away satisfactorily?
- Is there a holding tank? You need this for UK inland cruising or you will need to install a chemical toilet.

Equipment

Another aspect to consider is how many of the extras are included in the price? Most boats will have equipment and personal gear which may or may not be included in the asking price. Sometimes these become bargaining tools if negotiations otherwise grind to a halt. If, as most of us do, you are spending every last penny to buy your dream, you will find that you can often negotiate the price to include a selection of operational, even if not brand new, electronic wizardry which could make your life on board that much more pleasurable and manageable.

Nowadays you will find that the majority of British motor cruiser are constructed from fibreglass. Here a wooden wheelhouse has been incorporated into a fibreglass hull and cabin structure.

The hull

Having taken a good look around inside, take a broader look at the outside. With the structure of the boat, there is a different approach depending upon whether you are looking at fibreglass, wood, steel or aluminium.

Fibreglass

Fibreglass is also known as GRP (glass reinforced plastic) or FRP (fibre reinforced plastic). The commonest material from which motor cruisers are built these days is fibreglass. When introduced in the late 1940s and early 1950s it was thought that fibreglass was virtually indestructible and would last for ever. Surprisingly, the early boats constructed in fibreglass have stood the test of time well, but early hulls were laid up heavier and with more attention because fibreglass was such a new concept. As time has gone by, it has been found that

hull construction does not need to be as heavy to achieve satisfactory strength and lay up weights have generally been reduced. The most critical thing learned in the early days was that fibreglass construction requires the resin, which bonds the glass fibres together, to cure at a carefully controlled temperature to ensure

When viewing a fibreglass boat, look for tell-tale blisters in the hull – these may indicate the presence of osmosis which can be a very expensive problem to cure.

satisfactory bonding and strength. Most boats are laid up by hand or by hand-operated machines and are therefore very much dependent upon the skill of the operator and the correct levels of heat and humidity levels. It is really not possible for an amateur to determine how well a hull has been laid up. You need to bring an experienced surveyor onto the scene and leave it to him. A professional surveyor will also be able to check the construction for any degradation of older boats known as osmosis or the dreaded boat pox. As it ages, fibreglass is susceptible to the ingress of water through the outer skin of the construction known as the gel coat. Boats which are left in the water continuously, without the opportunity to dry out, are the most susceptible. The gel coat (or outer hull skin) becomes porous over time. Wintering the boat ashore every year allows some of the dampness which has been absorbed to dry out and delays the onset of osmosis.

As minute droplets of water squeeze through the porous gel coat, they get into the fibreglass strands and mix with any residue which may be left from the cured resin which was used in the construction of the hull. The water then reacts with this residue and forms an acidic solution which starts to attack the adjacent resin and also draws in more water. The mixture of water and acid then expands. This causes bubbles to form in the gel coat as it is the only way to relieve the pressure of acid and water which has now built up in the laminate. If untreated, eventually the hull becomes completely porous and loses its inherent strength. This is a serious problem. The only answer is to peel off the old gel coat and affected underlying laminate, open up any deep blisters, steam clean the whole area to remove the residues that caused the problem, dry with infra red lamps and finish with more steam cleaning. The hull is then filled, faired and

coated with epoxy. Any laminate which has been removed is replaced at the same time. A professional repair of this nature normally takes between a month and two months to complete and, being labour intensive, it is expensive. Make sure you get a surveyor to check for the level of moisture in the hull and give an opinion on its condition before agreeing to a purchase. This then is a very important aspect to take into account when buying a fibreglass boat and one which the layman will have difficulty in assessing himself.

You may not be able to detect osmosis but you can look for signs of laminate damage. Generally professional repairs to fibreglass are almost impossible to detect. Therefore if you are able to detect repairs by eye, it suggests that less care may have been taken of the boat than you might have hoped. Weaknesses in the construction often appear as craze fractures. These soon fill up with dirty rain water and, before long, become clearly visible. Generally they can be ground out, re-laminated and finished with a new gel coat layer so that the repair is as good or probably better than the original.

Wood

It is difficult for the untrained eye to see rotten wood. However you can definitely smell it, particularly if the boat has been shut up for a while. Rotting timber has a rather musty, sweet, sickly smell. The most common form of wood rot is likely to be caused by rain water leakage rather than underwater leaks. Nevertheless always look in the bilges for 'tide marks'. If a wooden boat has potential problems with her fastenings (the nails or rivets which hold the hull planks to the frames) she will leak. An owner who knows you are coming to look at his boat will always get there first to pump out. Look for the signs.

It is difficult to hide deck leaks without repainting. If the whole of the deckhead (ceiling) smells of new paint, it could be an indication that there is something to cover up. The most likely places to look for wood rot from the inside are the outer ends of the deck beams and possibly the top plank of the hull where it meets the deck and the adjacent covering board, the outermost deck plank, which is often cut around hull frames leaving many areas of end grain susceptible to water ingress leading to rot if the timber is not able to dry out.

There is no need to take a vicious spike or bradawl. Owners never like sticking sharp objects in their boat, so they will definitely not be amused by a total amateur digging in. Gently tap your way along the sides of the deck beams from the centre outwards with the handle of a bradawl or small pin hammer. If the timber is sound, it will have a strong resonant ring, however if it is suffering from wet or dry rot, it will make a dull thud. Have a tap around to see what you find. If the owner knows he has a problem, human nature is such that either he will try to distract you or else he will confess. Either way you stand a good chance of finding out.

Generally, the greatest threat to a wooden boat is not the water it floats in but the water which falls from the sky. Never forget this when having a serious look at a wooden boat. Looking for rain water leaks is one of the most important things that a prospective purchaser can do to help himself.

Steel

Steel is, in many respects, a strong and substantial option providing that speed is not at the top of your agenda. By their very nature, steel cruisers are heavy and it is unusual to find steel-hulled planing motor cruisers. There are one or two but not many.

The most likely deterioration will inevitably be rust. This is usually not

The idea of buying a classic wooden motor cruiser may be very appealing but restoring a hull like this which has been laid up in a yard for some years may become a labour of love or a complete nightmare. This carvel hull needs some planks replaced and all the caulking renewed to make her seaworthy.

A good example of how the sacrificial anode (top left) is doing its job of protecting the hull and sterngear from the effects of electrolysis.

37

The deck fittings on any second-hand boat tell a story. This poorly repaired stanchion fixing and surrounding cracking indicate possible water ingress plus the destablisation of the fitting itself. A repair like this could also indicate a lack of proper general maintenance on the boat.

difficult to spot unless the surface has been recently painted over, so look out for fresh paintwork. Often steel hulls are faired over with a coating of plaster so that the painter can get a more perfect finish than would be possible with plain steel. It is however possible that the thin layer of plaster could come loose from the steel plating. The hull will still look almost perfect but a rough passage will soon start to crack and remove the plaster and it is not an easy job to repair. If you get the opportunity, just tap the hull with your knuckle and see if it all sounds the same. If the plaster is loose, the noise of the taps will change as you move from sound to loose plaster. It is very unlikely that steel welds will fail, however electrolysis between the steel hull and stainless steel shaft and a bronze propeller is a potential hazard. This is controlled by a series of wasting or sacrificial anodes bolted to each part of the sterngear. It is vital that this system and its

electrical connections are kept in tip top condition and that the anodes *do* waste away as they are protecting the hull and sterngear from doing the same.

Very often a surveyor will be able to test the thickness of the hull at various points to ensure that it is still structurally strong. Points for the amateur to inspect include the bilges and where frames and stringers meet. If water is allowed to gather in puddles caused by the construction of the hull, deterioration will inevitably set in. Most steel boats corrode from the inside outwards where water collects or at the 'wind and water' interface just above and below the waterline. Whatever you do, do not go poking around with a bradawl or screwdriver in fresh water puddles within the hull as you may find a weak spot and go straight through with embarrassing consequences. It may be acceptable for a professional surveyor to discover a weak area whilst conducting a pre-purchase survey, but it is certainly not acceptable for potentially time-wasting fender-kickers to go around pushing screwdrivers through hull plating leaving the inevitable havoc behind them.

Aluminium

Much lighter in weight than steel but immensely strong, aluminium, like steel, needs to be kept from oxidising. It is also, like steel, susceptible to deterioration through electrolysis. It tends to be less common on motor cruisers but is often used on the hull and superstructure of large motor yachts where weight is to be kept to a minimum. It is joined by welding but requires higher temperatures, much more skill and specialised equipment than that required for welding steel. Aluminium oxidisation shows as a white powdery deposit often hidden under layers of paint. As with a steel hull, don't go round stabbing at the hull with a screwdriver – leave it to the professionals.

Trailers

Trailers are one aspect that you can have a good look at yourself. There is nothing worse than having a wheel bearing collapse after a long day out boating. Trailers probably suffer more abuse than any other part of a boat. They are expected to operate at high speed behind a car and then not complain about being plunged into cold, often salty, water and still perform to their optimum specification.

Wheel bearings, brakes and brake cables are the most susceptible to water damage. Greased wheel bearings do require a chance to cool down before launching and they definitely require to be stripped out and cleaned every year. The wheel bearings will all wear out in a similar period of time and if one has gone, the others will soon follow.

Brake cables and brake shoes are notorious for seizing up, so try releasing the hand brake (having chocked the wheels first) and see if the wheels free up.

Ask the owner about trailer maintenance, and if you are faced with a blank look, you can reckon that you will have to replace the wheel bearings and brake cables in the near future to enable you to drive without the worry of one of them failing. A failed wheel bearing at speed is sufficient to turn over the towing vehicle, so I am told; a sobering thought.

If the trailer has been left standing for any length of time without movement, you will see signs of cracking in the walls of the tyres. If you need to leave the trailer for long periods, block it up and take the weight off the tyres. Finally, look at the construction of the trailer, if it is galvanised (matt grey colour) it should do the job well, however if the framework and axle(s) show signs of rust, which many do, you may have to ditch it and start again. A new trailer for a cabin sports boat will cost £2,000-£3,000, so it is worth taking a close interest in the trailer when you view the boat.

6

What Will it Really Cost?

After your home, a boat is probably the most expensive item you will ever contemplate buying. The big difference is that we all need somewhere to live, but few of us actually *need* a boat. If you are going into boat purchase with the intention of making money out of it, you're in for a big disappointment. I have never yet met anyone whose accountant would agree that boat owning is a prudent investment. Of course you can offset some of your expenses by chartering or offering instruction if the boat is suitably equipped and certificated, but a boat owner would be optimistic to expect money to come rolling in. The only way that it is usually possible to make a small fortune out of boat owning is to start off with a large fortune.

After allowing for the cost of purchasing the boat there are various fixed and variable costs that you will need to take into account. It is advisable to make out a budget sheet of these costs *before* you decide to make a purchase. You don't want to put yourself right off the idea but on the other hand you really need to know what you are letting yourself in for in financial terms so there will be no nasty surprises.

Finance

If you are borrowing money to finance the purchase then you need to take into account monthly repayments and interest (see Chapter 7).

Moorings

Unless you can tow your boat and have a suitable storage space for it, you will almost certainly need to find a mooring. This could be a simple swinging mooring accessible by launch or dinghy, which is not terribly convenient but could cost as little as £100 per year. Swinging moorings are usually administered by local authorities or local yacht clubs who may offer a launch service to get you to your boat. There are often long waiting lists for the more inexpensive berths. You just need to persevere and eventually you will be successful. I have belonged to a particular yacht club for almost 30 years and have, at last, been allocated a berth in my club's marina which costs about one third of commercial rates.

A berth in a five star marina, with every facility you could dream of, will probably cost 10-15 times the cost of an unserviced swinging mooring. (See Chapter 8 for information on where to keep a boat.)

Insurance

Surprisingly, there is no obligation to have your boat insured. However most marinas in the UK, together with the British Waterways Board, do require your vessel to be covered against Third Party Risks as a minimum and, if you have borrowed money against the vessel itself, the finance company will almost certainly insist upon comprehensive cover.

The insurers may look more favourably on your policy if you have taken some boat handling courses and have gained some qualifications (Photo: Broom Boats).

Even if you are not obliged to insure, it does make common sense for peace of mind. The enormous range of risks to which a boat is exposed makes insurance a must in my book and you will be surprised at just how inexpensive it is. You should be able to negotiate an annual premium of somewhere between $^1/_2$ and 2 per cent of

the boat's value depending upon the age, size, value, speed and where she is going to be kept. This could become subject to a no-claims bonus as claim-free boating time ticks by. When you compare this cost to car insurance it is not expensive. I am currently paying almost 7 per cent of the value of my car in insurance and I haven't had a motoring claim for more than 20 years.

The underwriter will be very interested in where the boat is to be kept and the likely risks associated when you are not on board. Although an owner's level of experience is not the most important factor in assessing a risk, underwriters will always look upon a risk more favourably if an owner has gone to the trouble and effort to obtain even the most elementary qualification, together with some experience of handling the type of boat he is about to purchase.

What's covered?

Check your policy carefully to see what items on board are actually covered. Generally tenders, outboard motors and trailers are not covered by a boat policy unless they are marked with the vessel's name and added as individual items to make up the total insured value.

In commission

There is an agreed 'in commission' period which is when the boat is available for the owner's immediate use and a 'laid up out of commission' period which is when it is agreed that the boat will be laid up and not used. There are no restrictions on working or refitting the boat so long as she remains laid up. This is the period that she is either out of the water or immobile at her berth. If a major refit is undertaken, it is important to inform your broker as the cover you have may not include major refits.

Third party liability

Third party liability cover is important. The minimum you are likely to be offered is £1,000,000 in the event that something happens to your boat which affects other people or property. Policies for larger craft are likely to offer up to £2,000,000 third party cover.

Speed boat exemption clause

If the boat you are contemplating has a maximum speed in excess of 17 knots, your policy will be subject to a speed boat exemption clause. Whilst aimed particularly at speed boat owners, it also covers all other pleasure craft capable of more than 17 knots. You will not be covered for racing, leaving the boat moored unattended off an exposed shore, water skiing or aquaplaning. The latter two can be optionally covered.

Transit cover

If you are planning to trail the boat you will need transit cover but this will not provide third party cover in the event of the trailer becoming detached from the car. The Road Traffic Act specifies that this risk must be covered as part of the car policy.

Excess

You will be expected to pay an excess for each and every claim. This could be as low as £50 and as much as you consider sensible. The more you offer to pay, the less your premium will be. Your policy will not include charter as standard. Some vessels will not be assessed as suitable for skippered charter, particularly those capable of very high speed. If you ask for charter cover you will pay a higher premium and larger excess for the period of the charter.

Betterment

On most things we insure, we expect to have our losses repaired or replaced and if, as a result of the claim, we are better off, we think ourselves lucky. In marine insurance, the policy is likely to include a clause referring to allowances for 'betterment'. In realistic terms, if as a result of your claim, your boat is in better condition than it was before the claim, the insurance company is entitled to negotiate with you to reduce their liability by the amount that you are better off. So, if as a result of limited repairs to your hull, the entire hull has to be repainted to ensure a colour match, you are almost certain to be asked to make a contribution towards it because the hull is in much better condition after the claim than it was before. Equally if something happens to your radar which is covered by insurance and, because of technical advances, it can only be replaced by a more highly specified model, again you will be invited to make a contribution to cover the added value that the replacement offers. You will find that a wooden boat will cost more to insure than a GRP equivalent as it will be more costly to repair.

Insurance conditions

As a condition of marine insurance you will be expected to take all reasonable precautions to keep the vessel in a proper state of repair and at all times exercise due care in the protection, use and manning of the vessel. This means that if it can be proved that you have not followed the above paragraph to the letter, you may not be covered.

Registration

If your boat is registered either on Part I of the Registry of British Ships or Part III, the Small Ships Register (SSR), the registration will need to be renewed every five years. No reminders are sent out so don't forget. If you propose to venture abroad, you must have your boat registered on one of the above registers. Be aware that a vessel which is registered on Part I of the Registry of British Ships gives proof of legal title and records any financial charges registered over the boat but registry on Part III, the Small Ships Register, does not give this reassurance. Take care and remember the old legal

adage: 'caveat emptor' – let the buyer beware. For more information on registering boats and registration see Chapter 9.

Hull maintenance

Painting and varnishing

If your boat is constructed from timber in any form (other than a teak deck or trim), it will require regular painting or varnishing. This really does need to be done annually whether you use the boat a lot or not. If you try to make it last longer, you will inevitably end up with a much, much larger job to do later. The bottom of the boat will suffer from marine growth and need to be anti-fouled at least once a year. Whilst there are now copper based coverings which claim to last several years, my experience of conventional anti-foulings is that they really do only last one season. Get the job done in the spring ready for the active part of the season. A dirty bottom can slow you down by several knots, so a clean bottom can make a substantial saving on fuel costs.

Underwater

When the boat is lifted out to have the bottom anti-fouled, it is prudent to take apart and grease all the seacocks. These are the means of closing through-hull openings; in the event of an emergency, you may need to close one of them in a hurry and they will soon seize up if not operated on a regular basis.

If the boat is designed for salt water use, it will probably have a means of cathodic protection against the wasting away of dissimilar metals which are used in boat construction below the water line. There will be zinc anodes attached to the hull and wired internally to all metal fittings. These anodes *should* corrode away if the system is working correctly. If they do then it shows that the propeller(s), rudder(s), shaft(s) and other underwater metal fittings are being protected from erosion by electrolysis but they should be replaced before they have wasted away completely. If they don't waste away, get the installation checked as it is possible that the electrical circuit, of which they are part, may have been broken. The stern tube(s), through which the propeller shaft(s) pass, are fitted with watertight seals. These require regular attention to ensure that they remain in optimum condition and keep your boat afloat.

Engine servicing

It may seem obvious but it needs to be said that if you are going to rely solely on engines for propulsion, they need to be reliable. One way to ensure this is by having them serviced regularly. Unless you are a professional mechanic this is best left to a marine service agency or engineer. You will therefore have to allocate a fair sum for annual engine maintenance (a marine service agent will probably give you a guestimate of likely costs for servicing the engine of the boat you are contemplating buying). You can cut down on your costs by doing some of the routine maintenance tasks yourself. Regular checks should include the replacement of fuel filters, oil filters, engine oil, gear box oil, belts, anodes, topping up of batteries etc. If you opt for a diesel-powered boat, the RYA run a very useful course for beginners on diesel engine maintenance (for details see page 94).

The marine environment is hostile to most of the components of a boat so regular washing down with fresh water is needed to prevent salt deposits from building up. Regular use, too, will help prevent corrosion and seizing up of engine, hull and fittings and will, indirectly, save

you money. It is a good idea to monitor wear and tear in the form of a log book where you can keep a note of any defects which need remedying; this is important if you share the boat or charter it. Remember: prevention is always better than cure – the truth of that may come home to you one day when you are ten miles out to sea and the engine starts to cough and the weather is looking threatening.

Fuel

If you decide upon a powerful, spine shattering, water dragster, your greatest variable cost will inevitably be that of fuel. Even if you don't, fuel is one of the expenses which you will need to budget for. Before making your final decision on choosing a boat, the choice of fuel really does need to be taken into account.

In the UK, the tax on marine (red dyed) diesel is dramatically less than the garage pump diesel used in cars and lorries. The saving of around 75 per cent off garage pump prices makes the running costs of diesel-powered boats very attractive. The cost of petrol at marinas and boat yards is considerably more than garage pump prices because of the stringent regulations covering the storage of petroleum. This means that a litre of marine diesel could be as little as 20 per cent of the cost of a litre of petrol at a marina. In the mitigation of petrol, though, you will find that the cost of purchasing a petrol-driven boat will be less than the cost of one fitted with diesel engine(s) and that the resale value will be similarly affected. However, there may well be a better second-hand market for diesel rather than petrol. It's your decision and it needs to be taken carefully.

Recently LPG (liquefied petroleum gas) is starting to become available for boats. This requires a modification to the fuel

One of the pleasures of boat ownership is looking for fittings, equipment and other marine items to enhance life afloat. Boat shows are a good places to look for new or specialist equipment but boat jumbles are also excellent places to hunt for bargain boat bits.

tank, as it is stored under pressure, but its advantage is that it is similar in price to diesel. Only time will tell as to whether it becomes the norm for petrol-powered boats.

Licences

If your boat is fitted with a VHF radio, or any other radio transmitting equipment, a ship's radio licence will be required and needs to be renewed annually. The radio licence is just like a car tax disc and should be shown prominently on the port side of the vessel. The skipper or someone regularly on board will also need to complete a one day VHF operator's course and obtain a Short Range Certificate (SRC) before the set can be used. This is a once-only course offered by most RYA schools and does not need to be repeated.

For more information on radio licensing, contact The Radio Licensing Centre, Post Office Customer Management, PO Box 1495, Bristol BS99 3QS.

On certain rivers and estuaries, you may require a separate licence to enable you to keep your boat on and use the waterway. These can be quite expensive and vary from area to area. In coastal areas they are often included in the mooring fees but on inland waterways they are generally separate and quite substantial.

Essential equipment

If you plan to cruise extensively, along with kitting out the boat with creature comforts, you may need to upgrade the safety equipment you have on board. The RYA booklet *Cruising Yacht Safety* (*C8*) is a comprehensive guide as to what you should consider. The basics are given on page 34.

45

Exploring new creeks and harbours is the goal of most cruising folk. This motor boat is heading up Lymington river towards the visitors' berths in the marina.

Charts, almanacs and pilot books

If you intend to venture out of your home port, you will need a selection of navigation reference books and charts appropriate to the area. There are three main sources of charts. There is a vast world-wide range of Admiralty charts and publications including the new Small Craft Folios which have been designed with small boat users in mind and do not require an enormous chart table to use them. There are also navigation charts available from Stanfords and Imray, both of whom include a range of waterproof charts which the Admiralty does not currently provide.

You will find that once you get used to a particular style of chart, you will most likely stick with that type. Information for updating charts is published weekly, but it is unlikely that you will be organising your life around chart corrections. However, you need to be aware that because amendments are constantly being made, by the time you purchase a chart it will inevitably be out of date. So when you discover that a particular buoy isn't where you expected it to be, before you assume that you are lost, remember that navigational marks do get moved from time to time to take into account the movement of sandbanks etc.

Tidal information is available either in local tide tables or from a yachtsman's almanac. The latter has volumes of useful additional information and is highly recommended. You will need to replace it each year.

Visitors' moorings

A good guide to the cost of visiting other creeks and harbours is in the *RYA Marina Guide* booklet G8 which gives the cost of overnight stays away from your base port. Some marina operators offer free visits to other marinas within their group as part of your annual mooring fees.

Counting the real cost

As can be seen from the above, which can only be a guide, there are many costs involved in owning and maintaining a motor boat which may not be apparent when you first think that owning a boat might be a good idea. In round terms the annual cost of boat owning is likely to be 5-20 per cent of the boat's value with 10 per cent being a good place from which to start your budget calculations.

7

Raising the Necessary

Where can you go for a loan?

You only have to cast your eyes over any of the boating magazines to see that the boat loan market is lively and competitive. This is great news for the potential purchaser as it means that there is lots of competition and it is quite possible to shop around if you have the collateral.

There are a few independent specialist marine loan companies but the majority are subsidiaries of the big banking groups which specialise in the leisure boat market. They will be helpful in guiding you through the pitfalls of buying a boat, both new and second-hand, and will inevitably do their utmost to ensure that you get what you want, providing that they are happy that you can service their repayments. They will also have a much more arms-length view of your purchase and, if they don't want to lend you money against one particular boat or model but are happy to lend against another, don't ignore their advice. There will be a very good reason. They have a wealth of experience that you can't buy elsewhere.

There are various finance options available depending the type and value of the purchase ranging from a straight repayment loan up to about £20,000, to a fully-fledged marine mortgage with no fixed limit which can, subject to the realistic value of the security offered, include a residual value whereby you pay interest on the whole loan over the period but only repay a percentage of the capital involved. The great thing about boat finance is that there is a certain amount of flexibility allowed in formulating the agreement so you should have room to negotiate an arrangement that suits your requirements and financial limitations. The main players in this market are Bank of Scotland, Lombard Bank and Mercantile Credit.

Secured or unsecured loan or marine mortgage?

It is relatively easy to get an unsecured loan up to £7,500 with repayment periods up to ten years. A security is likely to be required for amounts over £7,500 but it is very unlikely that the boat itself will be acceptable as security unless it is registered under Part I of the Registry of British Ships. This effectively provides legal title to the boat and more importantly records any charges made over that title (see page 55). Generally your home, or a portion of it, will be required as the collateral for the purchase of an unregistered or SSR registered craft over £7,500. This may involve a second mortgage or re-mortgaging your home to include a surplus to pay for the boat and could be spread over a period longer than ten years. Your bank or building society will be able to advise on their policy on lending for this purpose.

A marine mortgage is a loan where the security is taken in part of the value of the boat. A minimum deposit of 20 per cent will be required and the repayment period spread over a period of up to ten years. As you can imagine, the finance company will suddenly take much more interest in the boat itself if you are considering a marine mortgage to ensure that their money is safely invested. They will inevitably require a structural survey report on a second hand boat and want to see the design and build specifications on a new one. If, for any reason, they are unhappy about lending you money against a particular boat, take heed and drop the idea. If they, with their vast experience of overseeing boat purchases, won't touch it, then you with little or no experience shouldn't either. If the loan goes ahead, it will take the form of a formal marine mortgage and a charge will be placed on the record of the boat's particulars on the Registry of British Ships to ensure that you do not run away and try to sell the boat to a third party without first paying off the mortgage.

Sharing the costs

It is not obligatory that a boat should have a *sole* owner. This opens up the option of sharing the use and the costs of owning a boat which could perhaps put motor cruising within your financial reach.

If the boat is registered on Part I of the Registry of British Ships it will be legally divided into 64 shares of ownership. So if you own it half and half with someone else, you will legally own 32 shares each.

Many, many boat owning partnerships just happen without any written agreements or legal involvement and go on for years and years without any problems. However, if you are contemplating boat sharing, it is always prudent to consider a simple written agreement covering:

- Title to the boat
- The means of settlement of all expenses and running costs

- How the agreement may be broken
- How the boat will be valued in the event of one partner wishing to withdraw
- Any restrictions about the transfer of a departing partner's share. This last point is usually the most difficult one.

Unless you have known your potential partner for a very, very long time and have the utmost faith in your continuing relationship, I would commend some sort of simple agreement for peace of mind on both sides. The most difficult problem is agreeing the value of the boat which is usually best done professionally, unless…

Sealed bids

Now there is a very canny solution which doesn't involve a professional valuation. The partner wishing to remain decides upon his valuation of his departing partner's share of the boat and places his bid in a sealed envelope. This is the amount that the remaining partner will offer his departing partner for his share of the boat. The departing partner has the option of either accepting the sealed bid or of reversing the deal and buying out the remaining partner for the amount he has just been offered. If the deal is reversed, the boat is sold and after the amount of the bid has been paid to the remaining partner, the departing partner keeps the balance of the sale. This ensures that the remaining partner will only bid an amount for his partner's share that he would himself accept for his own share. It sounds complicated but it is actually rather clever. This idea, I understand, was a brainwave of the well-known Scottish yachting writer, Michael Balmforth, who must have spent many happy hours during its conception. If you agree that this is an equitable solution, then details of it should be included in the initial agreement.

8

Where to Keep Your Cruiser

At home

If the boat you choose is less than 7.5m (24.5ft) or thereabouts, it may be possible to keep it at home and tow it to the launch site. Although from a purely cost point of view this may seem ideal, there are several points to consider.

- Can your existing car physically tow what may weigh in total 1000-2500kg (19.5-49cwt)?
- You should be aware that your car's fuel consumption when towing is likely to be reduced by 25-40 per cent.
- The top legal speed when towing is 60 mph so your journey will take longer than you may anticipate.
- Do you have sufficient suitable space at home to park the boat and trailer?
- If you are considering outside storage, are you likely to annoy your neighbours if their view is obstructed by a boat on a trailer? It will seem much very much larger ashore than it looks in the water especially if it is protected with a weatherproof cover.
- You will probably have to pay launch and recovery fees.
- Are you going to get frustrated waiting for your turn on the slip?
- How knowledgeable are you in manoeuvring a trailer behind a car? Reversing a trailer is not as easy as it looks especially if you cannot see where you are going.

In my long experience of towing, I reckon you should allow an extra 2-4 hours per outing if you have to tow, launch and recover – and I don't think that's necessarily because I'm not very good at it.

The RYA booklet ZW12, *Where to Launch Around the Coast*, is full of suitable slipway facilities ideal for trailer boating.

Swinging moorings and piles

Swinging moorings and piles are great to use as a visitor but, frankly, they are a bit of a pain when it comes to keeping a boat on them permanently.

Advantages
- The great advantage of swinging moorings and piles is the cost or lack of it. Swinging moorings will cost between 10 and 30 per cent of the cost of a marina berth for a similar size craft.
- They are generally managed by local authorities and yacht clubs and, because their upkeep is relatively inexpensive and their running costs are low, they are very economical in financial terms.

Disadvantages
- There are usually long waiting lists before a swinging or pile mooring becomes available.
- You can only get out to your boat by dinghy or launch. Some clubs and authorities offer a launch service during the summer but you will have to wait your turn.

Swinging moorings (above) and piles (below) provided by the local authorities are probably the cheapest option for cruiser owners but they do have their disadvantages. You will need a dinghy to reach your boat plus she is at the mercy of severe weather so you need to keep an eye on her. Also she could be vulnerable to theft so your insurance company may require extra security for outboard engines and want electronic equipment removed when the boat is unattended.

- There is no water or electricity available.
- There may be showers and toilets provided ashore but it is a major trek if you have the misfortune to be taken short in the middle of the night.

Dry berthing

Dry berthing is the service offered at some marine facilities which involves your boat being lifted out of the water using what can only be described as an enormous fork lift truck. They then stack her on a purpose-built rack ashore when it is not

51

If you opt for a marina berth for your boat you can probably expect water and electricity on the pontoon, 24 hour security, marina facilities such as showers, toilets, a restaurant and bar, slip and/or craning out facility, workshops, chandlery, and fuel plus free car parking. But all this comes with a fairly hefty price tag in most south coast marinas.

being used. This service costs about the same as a marina berth but because your boat is stacked in a rack when you are not using it, you don't have to worry about anti-fouling, dirty bottoms or damage from rubbing alongside pontoons or being hit by other boats whilst tied up in your berth. Providing the fork lift truck driver knows his business, your boat should be very safe indeed. From a security point of view, the racks are enclosed in protected compounds.

In an ideal world, you just phone up the day before, book your launch, then just turn up and drive your boat away. When you've finished your boating activities, you tie her up on the waiting pontoon, chuck the keys in the office and she is recovered, washed down and stacked on the boat

rack ready for next time. It sounds absolutely perfect.

There are, however, disadvantages to this system. You will have to give plenty of notice for busy weekends such as bank holidays and even then there may be delays. So spur-of-the-moment decisions to take the boat out may be impractical depending on how busy the yard is. You will not be popular if you continually forget to give sufficient notice to have your boat launched and just turn up expecting the staff to drop everything and look after you.

Also, the secure racks in which the boats are stacked, sometimes three or four high, are not generally accessible to owners so this is a restriction. You can only get to your boat when she is in the water.

Marina berths

The concept of marina berthing originated, not surprisingly, in the USA before the second world war. Convenience was the requirement and the concept of a pontoon where you could leave your boat safely moored up adjacent to all mod cons was considered the way forward.

It wasn't until the late sixties and early seventies that the first marinas started to appear in the UK and it was realised that, for a price, you could keep your boat in a purpose-designed facility with all mod cons included. You can expect free car parking, the provision of water and electricity on your pontoon, workshop facilities, slipway or lifting service, storage ashore during the winter, a chandlery, fuel, oil, 24 hour security, close circuit TV, toilets, showers, laundry, bar and restaurants, brokerage and waste disposal. None of this comes cheap as you can see from the table below.

Costs

It is always dangerous to try to quote prices in a book of this nature because of the widely differing geographical areas and facilities offered but, to give a rough guide (at year 2000 price levels), the amount you might expect to pay for a mooring is as shown below.

There may be opportunities for doing deals on an individual basis but that will depend entirely upon the availability of berths and your own negotiating skills.

There are also weekly and monthly rates which vary widely so I am not prepared to stick my neck out any further. You will find the *RYA Marina Guide* booklet G8 a help in being more specific. It lists over 250 marinas together with their mooring charges, number of berths, tidal access times, largest size accommodated and the facilities that they offer.

Size of craft	Swinging or pile mooring	Dry berthing	Marina price ranges
7.5m (25ft)	£75-250	£1500	£1100-£3200
10m (33ft)	£100-350	£2000	£1500-£4300
15m (50ft)	£250-400	n/a	£2200-£6400
20m (65ft)	£400-700	n/a	£3000-£8500

9

Registration

A boat, as we have seen earlier in the book, is probably your second most valuable possession after your home and yet there is no legal requirement for it to be positively distinguishable from another. Your third most expensive possession, your car, has its own registration plates and chassis number which makes it unique. Registration as a British Ship is a means of providing that uniqueness. There are two ways open to the yachtsman to register a 'British ship' with proper ship's papers, a certificate of registry and an official number. These are the Part I Register (previously known as The Register of Shipping) and the Part III Register, also known as the Small Ships Register (SSR). Both are now encompassed within the regulations of the Merchant Shipping Act 1995, and maintained up to date by the Registry of Shipping and Seamen at Cardiff in Wales. Address and contact details are in Appendix 9 – Useful Addresses and Contact Details.

Must I register?

There is no legal requirement in the UK that either the boat or the driver be licensed or registered. This gloriously British freedom is one shared less and less by our neighbours in Europe or the United States, New Zealand or Canada. Having said that, most boat owners choose the option of registering their vessel for a number of reasons.

If you intend to leave British territorial waters, your boat will need to be registered to fulfil the requirements of international law to sail on the high seas and to fulfil the laws of most of the countries into whose territorial waters you may choose to venture. The 1956 Geneva Convention on the High Seas provides that ships take the nationality of their owners, and requires individual states to issue documents which provide evidence of the ship's right to fly the flag of the owner's state whilst on the high seas (in our case that is outside British territorial waters) or the territorial waters of foreign states. As motor boats fall within the definition of a 'ship' as described in the UK Merchant Shipping Act 1995, the provisions of the convention apply as much to pleasure motor boats as to commercially operated vessels.

There are two options that a boat owner has to register his craft. The first is to apply for registration on either Part I of the Register, which is the part which also lists merchant ships, or Part III – previously known as the Small Ships Register (SSR).

The main difference between them in practical terms is that Part I provides evidence of title to the vessel and gives the facility for a charge to be registered against the title of the vessel if money is lent towards its purchase but Part III does not. This charge will only be lifted when the loan is paid off. This has obvious attractions to finance companies who offer loans in the form of marine mortgages using the equity provided by the vessel herself as security.

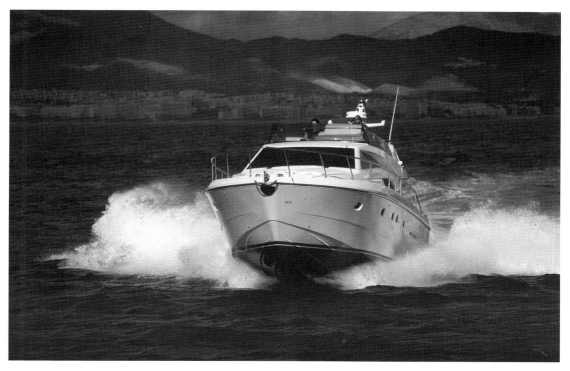

If you intend to leave British waters, your boat will need to be registered to fulfil the requirements of most European countries.

Part I requires a survey to measure the size of the vessel calculated in registered tons and a unique reference number and the registered tonnage is carved or fixed in such a way that it is difficult to remove from the vessel's main structure.

Part III (SSR) is a record of the details of the length, type, name and owner of craft which are declared by the owner at the time of registration and therefore open to inaccuracy and/or abuse. An SSR number is issued which is shown on the hull.

The SSR was established in 1983 to overcome the substantial costs involved in Part I Registration. In practical terms, however, there is little difference in the eyes of the Geneva Convention or those of a French or Dutch harbourmaster, between a British yacht with a Part III (SSR) Certificate of Registry and one which is

registered under Part I of the UK Merchant Shipping Act 1995; each is perceived to be as 'British' as the other. Both are fully valid throughout the world.

In both practice and in law, however, there are some differences. They stem in the main from the less formal documentation required to register on Part III (SSR).

Part I Registration

Part I registration requires evidence of title, going back at least five years before the date of application, and so, conversely, thus provides some evidence of title for buyers and provides a means of proving title when the boat comes to be sold.

The disadvantages of Part I Registration over opting for the simpler SSR are its cost which is likely to exceed £400, and greater

Port of Choice

You will have the opportunity of selecting a Port of Choice if you are registering on Part I for the first time or you have the opportunity of changing an existing Port of Choice on an existing registered vessel should you choose to do so. Not every port in the country is a Port of Choice. The following are those approved by the Registry for British Ships:

Aberdeen	Dartmouth	Kirkwall	Preston
Aberystwyth	Dover	Lancaster	Ramsgate
Alloa	Dumfries	Leith	Rochester
Arbroath	Dundee	Lerwick	Runcorn
Ardrossan	Exeter	Littlehampton	Rye
Ayr	Falmouth	Liverpool	Salcombe
Banff	Faversham	Llanelli	Scarborough
Barnstable	Felixstowe	London	Scilly
Barrow	Fleetwood	Londonderry	Shoreham
Beaumaris	Folkestone	Lowestoft	South Shields
Belfast	Fowey	Maldon	Southampton
Berwick-on-Tweed	Fraserburgh	Manchester	St Ives
Bideford	Glasgow	Maryport	Stockton
Blyth	Gloucester	Methil	Stornoway
Borrowstoness	Goole	Middlesbrough	Stranraer
Boston	Grangemouth	Milford Haven	Sunderland
Bridgewater	Granton	Montrose	Swansea
Bristol	Great Yarmouth	Newcastle	Teignmouth
Brixham	Greenock	Newhaven	Troon
Buckie	Grimsby	Newport	Truro
Burntisland	Hartlepool	Newry	Weymouth
Caernarvon	Hartlepool West	North Shields	Whitby
Campbeltown	Harwich	Padstow	Whitehaven
Cardiff	Hull	Penzance	Wick
Cardigan	Inverness	Peterhead	Wigtown
Chester	Ipswich	Plymouth	Wisbech
Colchester	Irvine	Poole	Workington
Coleraine	King's Lynn	Port Talbot	
Cowes	Kirkcaldy	Portsmouth	

You should therefore add the Port of Choice below your ship's name on the stern:

Saucy Sal

Weymouth

complexity. However, because Part I Registration investigates the recent ownership history of the vessel you should be confident that there are no nasty skeletons waiting to catch you out. Equally, when you come to sell, your prospective purchaser will have a similar assurance and this may help to encourage the sale. Part I Registration used to be a once-only procedure and valid for the life of the vessel. Now, however, like the SSR, Part I Registration is renewable every five years and again like the SSR the Certificate of Registry is now a laminated white card rather than the 'Blue Book' coveted by boat owners.

Registered tonnage and measurement survey

In addition to providing documentary evidence of title to the boat going back five years, you will be required to engage a surveyor from one of the eight approved classification societies to take the appropriate measurements and calculate the tonnage for the Register. This is not a condition survey and should not be viewed as such. It may however be possible to combine this measurement survey with a full condition survey, but the two must not be confused. In realistic terms, you are unlikely to think about registration at the time you ask for a full condition survey but if you do think that far ahead, you might save money. The measurement survey is in fact merely a matter of taking a handful of fairly crude measurements of the overall length of the boat, the interior volume of the main living space, making an allowance for machinery space and doing a simple calculation to an archaic formula to find the registered tonnage. Registered tonnage has nothing to do with the weight of the boat, but is derived from an 18th century method of estimating the volume of cargo a ship could safely carry. This tonnage was then used to levy fees such as

harbour and light dues on the vessel. If it was crude in the 18th century, you may wonder about its relevance to the modern pleasure boat in the 21st century. But for all the best bureaucratic reasons, its requirements remain the same for a motor boat as they do for a merchant ship. In fact, the process and the calculation are basically the same, but rather simpler in the case of a motor boat.

The carving note

The outcome of the measurement survey is the carving note. One condition of Part I Registration is that the ship's official number and registered tonnage is carved to the main beam of the vessel. Few modern boats have 'main beams' as such, or if they do, it is usually not sensible to try to carve anything into them. An alternative of a wood or metal plate is, therefore, carved with the ship's official number and her registered tonnage in tons and tenths of a ton and then permanently secured to the main beam or, in a steel, aluminium or glassfibre boat, to an equivalent position.

The cost of Part I Registration

In 2000 the total cost of Part I Registration was just over £400 including the £115 registration fee and travelling expenses of the surveyor required to do the measurement survey. The RYA has a list of surveyors who are qualified to perform this task on their behalf. Classification societies are listed in Appendix 9.

Until 1993 Part I Registration was a once-only task. The difficulty with this was that, once on a register, yachts (and ships) were never taken off and the records therefore became very inaccurate. In 1993 the regulations were changed to bring the Part I Registry into line with Part III (SSR) which is renewable every five years. The entire renewal was done automatically in 1994 when the original blue registration books became obsolete. This made 1999 the first year in which the entire Part I Register needed to be updated. It was hoped to remove those vessels which had long since disappeared and in doing so to reduce the number of yachts and pleasure craft on the register from about 45,000 to somewhere nearer a more accurate 20,000.

Part III Registration (Small Ships Register SSR)

Part III Registration is a simple self-registration system – that is to say that you fill in the forms yourself. Although there are penalties for making false statements, there are no independent checks on the information you provide, other than cross-checks once the application goes into the system. Because the SSR does not require any documentary proof of title when you apply, it cannot provide any documentary proof of title. If you buy a boat already on the Small Ships Register, the possession of an SSR number and certificate does not, of itself, provide any proof of title resting in the person offering to sell you the boat. Conversely, if you buy a boat not on the register and then put it on the register yourself, when you come to sell it the prospective buyer may ask for proof of title from you beyond the boat itself being on the register. It costs £10 to register a boat on the Part III Registry for a five year period.

There is no requirement, or indeed facility, when registering on the SSR to register a mortgage or other charge against the boat. This means that when you buy a boat with an SSR number, you have no way of knowing (at least through its registry) whether or not there might be a financial charge such as a mortgage still outstanding against it; and when you come to sell it you cannot prove by virtue of Part III registry that you are free and unencumbered to do so.

Part III Registration is restricted to:

- Vessels under 24m (78.7ft) in length which are privately owned

Part III Registration is NOT available to:
- Vessels over 24m (78.7ft) in length
- Vessels owned by a company
- Fishing vessels
- Submersible vessels

Part III Registration is only available to those who are ordinarily resident in the UK and who also fulfil one of the following requirements:
- British citizens
- Persons who are nationals of a European Union (EU) or a European Economic Area country (the EEA) other than the United Kingdom and are established in the UK.
- British Dependent Territories citizens
- British Overseas citizens
- Persons who under the British Nationality Act 1981 are British subjects
- Persons who under the Hong Kong (British Nationality) Order are British Nationals (Overseas)
- Commonwealth citizens not falling within those categories

Buying a boat already registered

If the boat you are buying is what is technically known as 'previously owned' she may already be on either the Part I Register or the Part III. If she is on the latter, the existing registration is immediately invalidated at the time of the sale and she must be re-registered with your own details. When you come to do this, the registration document will ask for details of the previous owner and the boat's previous SSR number, so it is important that you make sure that you get this information with any other papers at the point of sale.

If the boat is registered on Part I of the Registry of British Ships you contact the

Registry and apply to transfer ownership to you by providing the Bill of Sale, a Declaration of Eligibility and a fee of £69.00. If, however, the person from whom you are buying the boat (the vendor) did not re-register the yacht in his own name when he purchased it, you may have unwittingly acquired yourself a problem. Assuming there are no questions over the validity of your vendor's title to the boat, between the two of you, you will have to trace the last recorded registered owner and provide Bills of Sale in the favour of each subsequent owner up to and including your vendor. If this proves impossible (as is quite possible) you will either have to wait five years before re-registering the boat in your own name, or make a formal application to the High Court for an order requiring the Registrar to transfer the title. This could prove expensive as well as very time-consuming.

Buyer beware

As we have already seen, an advantage of buying a boat that is already on the Part I Register is that you will readily know if

Boatmark scheme

In 1995, in response to numerous cases of finance fraud, and also to discourage the theft of yachts and yacht equipment, the British Marine Industries Federation (BMIF) set up the Boatmark scheme in collaboration with a company called HPI Equifax. This company runs the anti-fraud database for the motor trade and has something like 20 million vehicles in its various motor car schemes, so it has wide expertise in fighting fraud.

When Boatmark was established, it was hoped that all finance agreements on yachts in the UK would be recorded and information made readily available to potential purchasers. Unfortunately, this has not happened as quickly as had been hoped, partly because finance houses were slow to embrace the scheme. Therefore just because no charge is registered, it does not absolutely guarantee that no charge exists.

The Boatmark scheme is based upon using the Hull Identification Number (HIN) introduced by the BMIF in the mid-80s to provide every boat in the country with a unique identifying code number. Each boat has its number clearly marked on the transom, either during construction or at some subsequent stage of its existence by one of over a hundred marking stations around the country. This HIN becomes the key identifier for the record of that particular boat which Boatmark maintains in a database linked to the national police computer.

The boat's keeper receives a certificate showing details of the boat, the HIN, the date of registration with Boatmark, and the name and address of the keeper. The record also notes any charges over the equity of the boat which have been registered. When the boat is sold, prospective buyers are able to confirm the validity of the information on the certificate by simple phone enquiry and this gives sellers a means of demonstrating whether a charge has been registered with the Boatmark scheme.

Registration under the Boatmark scheme costs £30. If you are buying a Boatmarked craft, especially if doing so privately, you can, for a modest search fee, have Boatmark check the number for you and ensure that no charges have been registered. Indeed, a Boatmark number will help you check the seller's title to the boat and many police forces are increasingly using Boatmark to report stolen craft. Let's hope it becomes universally accepted in the UK for all our sakes. Further details from Boatmark Ltd, telephone: 01722 413346.

there are outstanding financial charges, such as a mortgage registered against the boat. Conversely, because the Small Ships Register does not offer the facility for charges against the boat to be registered, an SSR number is of itself no proof at all that the boat is unencumbered. During the late 80's there were a number of cases of mortgages being offered to people whom, with the benefit of hindsight, a prudent lender might have declined. When some of these owners hit financial difficulties in the 1990s, they sold their boats, in many cases, without telling their buyer the entire financial story. The new owners then found themselves having to deal with finance companies who were still owed money and who had a mortgage charge against the boat. The unwary buyer, although with right on his side, found himself losing his boat to the previous owner's finance company. The moral of the story is to ensure as positively as you possibly can that the boat you are purchasing is unencumbered otherwise you could be the one who ends up lumbered.

10

Value Added Tax

Value Added Tax (VAT) was introduced in the United Kingdom in place of Purchase Tax on 1 April 1973. Since then VAT should be paid on any boat built in, or imported into, the European Union (including the United Kingdom) for private use.

The resale of a boat does not attract more VAT provided that:

- the owner is not a VAT-registered person or trader;
- the owner is buying the boat from another private individual who is not VAT registered;
- the boat itself has VAT-paid status.

This applies even if the purchase is through a broker whose turnover may require him to be registered for VAT. In this event the broker will charge the seller VAT on his sales commission – but that is for the seller to settle. However, if the purchase is made from the brokerage office of a boat builder who has taken the vessel in part-exchange against the sale of a new boat and is now selling it on, VAT may apply on the sale price. It is therefore important to establish whether the sale price which is being discussed is inclusive of VAT. It is now against the law in the UK for prices of goods liable for VAT to be quoted ex-VAT when being offered for private sale. However this regulation does get flouted on the pretext that boats are not always bought by private individuals, but may also be bought by VAT-registered companies or by non-EU residents, both of whom might be in a position to reclaim the VAT. This is particularly noticeable at

boat shows, the worst offenders being those who are acting as agents for overseas builders. So if you are looking at a new boat, clarify whether the price you are discussing is VAT inclusive or VAT exclusive.

Although VAT is not generally involved in a private sale within the United Kingdom on a boat built in the United Kingdom, the question of whether VAT has been paid on your boat (and whether you are able to prove it) is becoming increasingly important as the European Union (EU) moves steadily towards being a unified community for tax and customs dues. If it is intended to take the boat abroad, it is prudent to ensure that you are able to produce documentary evidence either that VAT has been paid on the boat, or that VAT is deemed to have been paid.

This means that when you come to buy your first motor cruiser, the seller must provide you with the original VAT receipt for the boat, if she was new after 1 April 1973 or, if she has been imported, evidence that VAT was paid at the time of importation or that relief was granted by the Customs authorities.

Alternatively, if she was built or, more correctly, first used in the UK before 1 April 1973 you will need the original sales invoice or builder's certificate showing the date she was first supplied within the EU. This is important to obtain as if the boat has changed hands outside the EU she will have lost her VAT paid status.

Unless the seller is able to produce proof that VAT on the yacht has been paid, either in the United Kingdom or elsewhere in the EU, or that other documentation exists to prove VAT status, you may find yourself facing a VAT assessment on the current value of the boat if an EU Customs official carries out a spot check. In the absence of all else, at least carry with you the Bill of Sale showing that the yacht was bought by you, a private UK resident, from another private UK resident and therefore whether or not VAT has been paid is solely a matter for British Customs jurisdiction.

Changes in legislation on exportation

Until the end of 1992 it was quite possible for a yacht built for a UK resident to be exported immediately upon completion without payment of VAT, for use elsewhere in the EU on a tax-free basis. The International Convention on Temporary Importation provided that all countries included in this agreement should permit the free use of recreational equipment and means of transport for tourist purposes for a minimum of six months in any one year. This rule was interpreted liberally in most European countries including France, Spain and Italy, and over the years tens of thousands of yachts built for northern European owners enjoyed tax-free status in Mediterranean marinas.

On 1 January 1993 the introduction of the European Single Market ended these concessions between EU States. Apart from a few months' grace for yachts already enjoying rights of temporary importation, VAT must be paid on any yacht in an EU State, owned by a resident of any EU State for his private use.

Also on 1 January 1993 a concession was introduced for any yacht in temporary importation within the EU on that day and taken into use as a pleasure vessel on or before 1 January 1985. Therefore, unless

you are able to prove either that the boat is VAT paid or that she was built before 1 January 1985 and was in EU waters at midnight on 31 December 1992, you will be liable to pay VAT on the current value.

VAT regulations are intricate, and regularly subject to change and fresh interpretation and you will frequently find that anything written about them is out-of-date as soon as it appears on paper. If the VAT-paid status of your first motor cruiser is not readily apparent from the original documentation which the seller can show you, and hand over to you on completion of the sale, then you need expert advice on the specific case of the boat you are considering. This should be available from your local HM Customs and Excise office or, if you are a RYA member, the RYA Cruising Department at RYA House in Eastleigh, Hants are highly knowledgeable and helpful on this difficult and complex matter.

VAT guidelines

The RYA draw your attention to the following guidelines:
- If a pleasure boat is sold outside the EU it automatically loses its VAT status.
- If you are buying a boat from a VAT registered organisation, VAT must be accounted for at the time of that sale.

There are two ways that a vessel can be granted relief from VAT:
- Returned Goods Relief: where a person takes a VAT-paid boat out of the EU and then returns with it at a later date but where it has not changed hands in the meantime.
- Change of Residence Relief: where the owner of a boat moves his residence from outside the EU to inside the EU and keeps the boat for his own personal use. However there are strict regulations

regarding timing. Details are given in HM Customs and Excise Notice 8.

The temporary importation into the EU of a boat registered outside the EU and owned by persons resident outside the EU is allowed so long as it is not lent, hired, sold or used as security inside the EU, in which case VAT will become due immediately in the country where the transgression takes place.

In 1998, HM Customs and Excise produced a two-page fact sheet especially intended for UK yachtsmen (both motor and sail) who have concerns about VAT. A transcript is published with this book as Appendix 5. Additionally you may find helpful the HM Customs and Excise Notice 8 which is entitled Sailing your pleasure craft to and from the United Kingdom and is available from your local HM Customs and Excise Office.

11

Motor Boat Training

No RYA book on boating would be complete without mention of appropriate training. The very comprehensive RYA training scheme for motor boaters is admired to the extent that many professional seamen working in sailing and motor yachts throughout the world travel to the UK to qualify for RYA/DoT Certificates. Certificates are awarded for vessels up to 24m (78.7ft) in length and successful completion represents a significant achievement in terms of competence.

Training courses

RYA training courses are available at three main sources:
* Local authority evening classes
* Commercial RYA training schools
* Selected yacht clubs

All RYA-recognised teaching establishments go through stringent inspections of their premises, facilities and the standard of instruction. Only those which pass these continuing assessments are able to issue RYA certificates and call themselves RYA Recognised Teaching Establishments. Look for the distinctive logo to be sure of the standard of course you may expect.

The initial RYA motor cruising course, An Introduction to Motor Cruising which is a very basic informal course run by some clubs and a few professional schools.

The more usual entry level for motor boaters is Day Skipper which is sub-divided into two parts. The shorebased training, which, as it suggests, centres around classroom teaching, provides an excellent background to the information you will need to know before heading out of harbour on a daylight cruise in familiar waters. It normally takes 20-30 two or three hour sessions of evening classes and the majority of courses are held from September to March. More recently some of the professional RYA schools have started to offer a condensed 5 or 6 day shorebased course covering the same syllabus but its time constraints mean that it has to be conducted at a very brisk pace which is hard work for both students and instructors alike. However it does offer an option to those who are unable to reliably commit one evening a week for 20–30 weeks.

The Day Skipper Practical Course, which is normally 5 consecutive days, involves living on board. The course will cover all aspects of running the boat, together with simple navigation and boat handling techniques. Navigating a small motor cruiser in a choppy sea is a totally different experience from doing the same on a stationary classroom desk.

The next level, Coastal Skipper, which takes a similar time to complete but requires an altogether more advanced level of competence. Those who have completed the Day Skipper Shorebased and Practical courses should have achieved the basic entry level requirement for Coastal Skipper. Whilst it is not impossible to enter the RYA scheme directly at Coastal Skipper level and miss out Day Skipper, unless you have a depth of previous experience, you would be advised against it. In any case, the enrolment evenings for RYA courses are specifically designed to allow you and your instructor to meet and to discuss your experience and to get you on the right course. Even having enrolled, it is not too late to change course, and I have had students who, after the first couple of sessions, are obviously not going to cope with the pace and have transferred to another class. You will find that very often the Day Skipper and Coastal Skipper evening classes are held on the same night which makes transfers easy.

The syllabus for both RYA shorebased classes is the same for both sailors and motor boaters. Sometimes motor cruising students find that their instructors are totally sailing-orientated and really do not understand some of the different problems faced by motor boats. It would, therefore, be prudent to ask your instructor what practical experience he has had in motor boats and how many other motor boaters are going to be on the course before enrolling.

Before taking your newly acquired boat to sea, you will need some training in handling and seamanship. You can join a club, go out with other members on their boats and learn through club courses or learn on your own boat at a sea school with a professional instructor.

Here a navigation pupil is comparing a paper chart with a radar image.

Cruising abroad on inland waterways

Some European countries, including France, Holland and Belgium, require the skippers of vessels cruising on inland waterways, to hold the International Certificate of Competence. You can obtain this from the RYA by submitting evidence that you have successfully completed one of the recognised DoT/RYA practical courses (see also Appendix 8) or by taking a test at an approved RYA ICC Test Centre.

RYA membership and publications

The Royal Yachting Association is not only the issuing authority for British Motor Cruising Certificates of Competence, some of which they issue on behalf of the Department of Transport, they are also the UK's largest representative for the sport of yachting – both sail and power. They reflect the views of more than 80,000 personal members and, being independent of government, are able to represent their members' views impartially.

In addition to their representative role, the RYA publish and market a range of

HM Coastguard Yacht and Boat Safety Scheme

Every year the Coastguard receive over 1000 calls from anxious relatives and friends reporting overdue small craft or distress calls from the boat's crew but often the rescue services are given little information about the boat. The Coastguard maintain a database to aid search and rescue operations. You can register with this scheme free of charge by contacting the Maritime Rescue Centre for your area (look under Coastguard in your phone book); they will send a brochure with a card for you to fill in with the following details:

- Owner's address and telephone number
- Details of shore contact
- Name of any relevant club or association
- Name of craft
- Type of craft
- Sailing or fishing number
- Description of boat
- Base or mooring
- Details of usual activity ie cruising, fishing, diving
- Details of radio and call sign and other equipment

- Type of distress signals carried
- Dinghy type
- Life raft type
- Lifejackets

Once you have filled in the details, send it to the Maritime Rescue Centre for your usual cruising area and they will store the details on computer and hard copy. In the event of an emergency, once you have given your boat's name (spelled correctly) the rescue services will then have instant access to this vital information to provide assistance. If you cruise out of your area, notify the local Coastguard station by radio of your purpose and destination as usual and let them know you are registered with scheme CG66.

books and booklets which are available to members at advantageous rates. RYA membership is well worth serious consideration if you are contemplating getting into motor boating. Contact them on 023 8062 7400 for more information. Appendix 7 gives details of useful publications for the first time boat owner and Appendix 8 gives details of the RYA motor cruising training schemes.

BMIF/RYA Boat Building Contract

BuildNumber/Hull Identification No./boatmark No.

THIS AGREEMENT is made the ___ day of ____ ____

BETWEEN:

1. [_____] a limited company incorporated in England (Reg.no No.)/ Scotland (Reg.no. No.)/Northern Ireland (Reg.no. No.)/ a sole trader/a partnership whose registered office/principal place of business is [_____] ("the Builders")

AND

2. [_____] ("The Purchaser")

jointly ("The Parties")

---

1 Agreement and specification of the boat

1.1 The Builders agree to construct and the Purchaser agrees to buy the boat described in the Specification as set out in Schedule 1, together with any drawings and plans, all of which shall be signed by the Parties, ("the Boat") and in accordance with the terms of this Agreement.

1.2 Subject to any agreed amendments to the Specification, drawings and plans, the Purchaser shall have the right to reject any workmanship, materials and/or equipment which does not comply therewith. Such rejection shall be in-effective unless confirmed to the Builders by notice in writing within 14 days.

1.3 The Builders shall be under no contractual or other obligation to accept any order of the Purchaser until it has been confirmed and signed on behalf of the Builders by their authorised representative.

1.4 The Builders shall build the Boat in compliance with all applicable statutory requirements and regulations relating to the construction and sale of the Boat in the European Union or any other requirements or regulations which may be agreed in writing between the Parties.

2 Modifications and changes to the specification

2.1 No modifications or changes to the Specification, Delivery Date and/or price shall be binding on the Parties unless and until set out in writing and signed by both Parties.

2.2 The Builders shall have the right to refuse to agree to any modification or change to the Specification or Plans.

3 Contract price and payment

3.1 The price of the Boat is the amount set out in Schedule 2 together with the cost of any modifications or changes to the Specification agreed between the Parties under Clause 2.1 and any adjustments made under Clause 3.3 and, if applicable, VAT at the rate applicable from time to time (together "the Contract Price"). The Purchaser agrees to pay the Contract Price by instalments as set out in Schedule 2 ("Stage Payments") and as provided in this Clause.

3.2 The Builders shall give the Purchaser 14 days' notice of the anticipated date of completion of each stage of construction as provided in Schedule 2. On expiry of such notice the Purchaser shall certify that the stage has been satisfactorily completed (such certification not to be unreasonably withheld) whereupon the relevant Stage Payment will become immediately due and payable in full without discount, deduction or set off.

EITHER *Delete one of the alternatives to Clause 3.3 (see Notes for Guidance)*

3.3 If during the period of this Agreement there is an increase in the Builders' net cost of constructing the Boat, whether in relation to materials or labour or which arises from any change in the applicable law or regulations, and provided always that the Builders have proceeded with reasonable despatch, the Parties agree that the Builders shall be entitled to increase the Contract Price proportionately to such increase in cost and the Purchaser undertakes and agrees to pay the Contract Price as so adjusted.

OR

3.3 Save as provided in Clauses 2.1 and 3.1 the Contract Price shall not be subject to any increase.

3.4 If the Contract Price is varied in accordance with Clauses 2.1 and/or 3.1 the Builders shall be entitled to require payment of any increase in the Contract Price by reason of any modification or change in full at the time of agreement thereto or, at their option, to receive such increase by way of additions to the Stage Payments.

3.5 If the Contract Price is varied in accordance with Clause 3.3 the amount of the increase shall be divided by the number of remaining Stage Payments and the amount so calculated shall be added to each remaining Stage Payment and Schedule 2 shall be amended accordingly.

3.6 If for any reason any tax, levy, charge or any other sum required to be paid by law shall be omitted from the amount of the Contract Price or shall be varied or introduced after the date of this Agreement and shall be required to be paid by the Purchaser the Purchaser shall pay such additional sum forthwith on demand.

4 Unpaid instalments

4.1 If the Purchaser fails for any reason to pay the full amount of any Stage Payment or other sum due to the Builders on the due date the Builders shall be entitled to stop construction of the Boat until all outstanding payments have been paid in full, and the Delivery Date shall be extended by the period of such delay in payment.

4.2 If such failure to pay any sum due continues for 14 days the Builders shall thereafter be entitled to charge interest at 4% over Barclays Bank plc base rate, or the Builders' current commercial overdraft rate if higher, after as well as before judgement, calculated from the date upon which such payment became due and payable.

4.3 After *a further* period of 14 days' delay the Builders shall, without prejudice to any other rights, be entitled:

4.3.1 to require payment from the Purchaser forthwith of the balance of the Contract Price then outstanding and to complete the construction of the Boat; or

4.3.2 to terminate this Agreement and to sell the Boat pursuant to Clause 10.2.

4.4 The Purchaser shall in addition be liable for any loss or damage, special, direct, indirect and/or consequential losses incurred by the Builders as a result of the delay in the payment of the Stage Payments or any other sums due hereunder.

5 Acceptance trial and delivery

5.1 The Boat shall be completed and ready for delivery at the place and on the date stated in Schedule 3 or on such later date as may be determined in accordance with the terms of this Agreement ("the Delivery Date").

5.2 Unless otherwise agreed between the Parties the Boat shall at the Builders' expense be taken on a trial trip (of not more than [   ] hours' duration) before delivery (the "Acceptance Trial"). The Builders shall give the Purchaser at least 14 days' written notice of the place and approximate duration of the Acceptance Trial, but if the date shall not be convenient to the Purchaser the Parties shall agree an altenative date not more than one month after the date proposed by the Builders.

5.3 If during the Acceptance Trial any defects in workmanship or materials or deviations from the Specification are found, the Builders shall forthwith rectify such defects or deviations and shall carry out a further Acceptance Trial in accordance with Clause 5.2.

5.4 If the Purchaser fails to attend a first Acceptance Trial, the Builders shall carry out a further Acceptance Trial pursuant to Clause 5.2 save that the cost thereof shall be for the account of the Purchaser.

5.5 If the Purchaser fails to attend such further Acceptance Trial, or if the Parties shall fail to agree an alternative date for a first or further Acceptance Trial, the Builders shall confirm in writing to the Purchaser that an Acceptance Trial has been deemed to have taken place and provided that the Builders shall certify that the Boat is

constructed in accordance with the Specification and performs satisfactorily the Purchaser shall be deemed to have accepted it.

5.6 At the satisfactory conclusion of the Acceptance Trial the Purchaser shall sign the Certificate of Delivery and Acceptance in the form provided in Schedule 4. The final balance of the Contract Price shall become due and payable immediately upon signature of the Certificate of Delivery and Acceptance or upon provision by the Builders to the Purchaser of the Certificate referred to at Clause 5.5 or upon the Purchaser's wrongful failure or refusal to sign the Certificate of Delivery and Acceptance.

5.7 The Purchaser shall take delivery of the Boat immediately upon signature by the Purchaser of the Certificate of Delivery and Acceptance and payment of the final balance of the Contract Price and any other sums owing to the Builders by the Purchaser. If the Purchaser fails to take delivery of the Boat or fails to pay any outstanding sums due to the Builders then, in addition to any other rights which the Builders may have, the Builders shall be entitled to require the Purchaser to pay such reasonable berthing and/or storage charges as the Builders shall notify to the Purchaser together with any other expenses reasonably incurred by the Builders, including but not limited to insurance, maintenance and lifting of the Boat in or out of the water until actual delivery shall take place.

5.8 The Purchaser and the Builders expressly agree that the Builders shall not be responsible for investigating or otherwise ensuring that the Purchaser is competent and experienced in the proper control and/or navigation of the Boat. The Royal Yachting Association will if requested by the Purchaser provide a list of boat handling/training establishments

6 Delays and extensions of time (force majeure)

6.1 If construction of the Boat is delayed directly or indirectly due to any cause beyond the Builders' reasonable control the Delivery Date shall be extended by the period of time during which such delaying event operates.

6.2 The Builders shall give the Purchaser written notice of any event in respect of which the Builders claim to be entitled to an extension of time:

6.2.1 within 7 days of its commencement, stating the date on which the delay commenced, the cause of it and its estimated duration; and

6.2.2 within 7 days of its end, stating the date on which it ended and the total period of the extension sought.

Any dispute arising between the Parties as to the operation of a delaying event shall be adjudicated in accordance with Clause 14.1.

6.3 If the Builders' premises, plant, machinery or equipment shall be so damaged by the operation of a delaying event for which the Builders are not responsible so as to make it impracticable for the Builders to complete the construction of the Boat, the Builders may, at their option (to be exercised within 21 days of the operation of the delaying event), cancel this Agreement by notice in writing to the Purchaser, whereupon the Purchaser shall be entitled by written election either:

6.3.1 to take over and complete the Boat without further liability on the Builders whereupon the Purchaser shall pay to the Builders all sums then due, whether by way of Stage Payments or otherwise; or

6.3.2 to require repayment of all instalments paid by the Purchaser to the Builders and upon such repayment title in the Boat and all materials and equipment appropriated to the Boat shall revest in the Builders.

7 Access to boat and to builders' premises

7.1 The Purchaser shall have the right to inspect the progress of construction of the Boat from time to time during the Builders' normal business hours with the prior written consent of the Builders, such consent not to be unreasonably withheld provided always that the Builders shall be entitled to appoint a representative to accompany the Purchaser or Purchaser's agent and that access shall extend only to those parts of the Builders' premises necessary for the inspection of the Boat and/or the materials and equipment appropriated thereto.

7.2 The Purchaser shall observe all current rules and regulations applied by and to the Builders, and to their premises.

8 Warranties

In addition to the Purchaser's statutory rights the following warranties shall apply:

8.1 Subject to the conditions set out below and otherwise expressly set out herein the Builders warrant to the Purchaser that the Boat will be of satisfactory quality and reasonably fit for the purpose(s) made known to the Builders in writing prior to the date of this Agreement whether or not such purpose is one for which the Boat is commonly supplied and will correspond with the Specification and any variation, addition or modification thereto. The Builders further warrant that the Boat will be free from defects in materials and workmanship for a period of 12 months from the time of delivery.

8.2 The Builders warrant to the Purchaser that on delivery the Boat uill comply with:

8.2.1 all legislative requirements and regulations relating to the sale of the Boat in the European Union for any purpose(s) made known under 8.1 above; or

8.2.2 any other requirements or regulations which may be agreed in writing between the Parties.

8.3 The Purchaser's statutory rights and the warranties set out in Clause 8.1 and 8.2 shall be subject to the following conditions:

8.3.1 The Builders shall have no liability for any defect in the Boat arising from the Specification supplied, provided or varied by the Purchaser;

8.3.2 The Builders shall repair or replace any defect in the workmanship, materials or equipment or their failure to correspond with the Specification. Such repair or replacement shall be carried out by the Builders at their premises or, where that is not convenient to the Parties, the Builders shall pay the reasonable cost of having the work carried out elsewhere;

8.3.3 The Builders shall only be liable for any defects or failures which were not apparent on reasonable inspection during the Acceptance Trial or within a reasonable time thereafter;

8.3.4 The Purchaser shall notify the Builders in writing immediately on discovery of any alleged defect and the Builders or their agent shall have the right to inspect the Boat including the right to carry out sea trials to enable the Builders or their agent to examine or assess the extent of the alleged defect. The expense of any such trials shall be borne by the Builders if the defect is shown to be one of workmanship or materials.

9 Insurance

9.1 The Builders shall insure the Boat (together with all equipment and materials installed or intended for it and within the Builders' premises) in the joint names of the Builders and the Purchaser from the date of this Agreement until the date of delivery.

9.2 Such insurance shall be effected with a reputable insurer for a sum equal to the replacement cost of the completed Boat (to a maximum of 125% of the Contract Price) and shall include the cost of any additions or variations to the Specification agreed between the Parties.

9.3 Such insurance shall be on terms no less favourable than the Institute Clauses for Builders' Risks *applicable* from time to time. Documentary evidence of such insurance, its terms and conditions and proof of payment of the premium shall be provided to the Purchaser on request.

9.4 In the event that the Boat, equipment or materials sustain damage at any time before delivery any monies received in respect of the insurance shall be receivable by the Builders and shall be applied by them in making good such damage in a reasonable and workmanlike manner and the Delivery Date shall be extended by such period as shall be reasonably necessary to effect the necessary repairs. The Purchaser shall not be entitled to reject the Boat, equipment or materials on account of such damage or repairs or to make any claim in respect of any resultant depreciation save that where the Boat is declared an actual or constructive total loss the Purchaser shall have the option, to be exercised within 28 days of the loss, of cancelling this Agreement *in which event the insurance money to the value of Stage Payments already paid shall be paid direct to the Purchaser by the insurers* and the Purchaser will abandon all rights under the said insurance to the Builders. This Agreement will thereupon be determined in all respects as if it had been duly completed and the Purchaser shall have no further right to claim against the Builders.

9.5 If the Builders fail to provide satisfactory evidence of insurance in accordance with the provisions of this Clause, the Purchaser shall be entitled to insure on comparable terms and to deduct the amount of the premium actually paid from the Contract Price.

10 Termination

10.1 The Builders shall be entitled to terminate this Agreement by written notice without prejudice to any other rights or remedies available if:

10.1.1 the Purchaser becomes insolvent;

OR

10.1.2 the Purchaser has failed without good reason to make one or more Stage Payments or any other payment within 28 days of such payment being due and payable and has not referred the underlying reason for such delay to dispute resolution under the provisions of Clause 14.

10.2 If the Builders exercise their right to terminate this Agreement under Clause 10.1 they shall be entitled to sell the Boat, the materials and the equipment and/or any other property of the Purchaser in the possession of the Builders for the purpose of the construction of the Boat. The Builders shall give the Purchaser 28 days' written notice of their intention to sell the Boat and/or other property and such notice shall give details of the reasons for the sale including details of any sums due and payable to the Builders together with details of the proposed method of sale. Following the sale of the Boat and/or other property the Builders shall repay to the Purchaser the balance of the proceeds of sale after deduction of all sums owing to the Builders and all reasonable legal or other expenses including, but not limited to, the costs of sale and maintenance and storage charges incurred by the Builders.

10.3 In addition to any other rights set out herein the provisions of the Torts (Interference with Goods) Act 1977 ("the Act") shall apply in relation to uncollected boats and/or other property and for the purposes of the Act it is hereby expressly agreed that the Builders' obligations to the Purchaser as custodians of the Boat and/or other property terminate upon the expiry or lawful termination of this Agreement and pursuant to the Act the Builders have a right of sale exercisable in certain circumstances as set out in the Act.

10.4 For the purposes of Clauses 10.2 and 10.3 only the Purchaser hereby irrevocably appoints the Builders as the agent of the Purchaser for the sale of the Boat and/or other property. The Purchaser shall co-operate with the Builders insofar as may be necessary to effect a sale of the Boat including signing or confirming any authority or instructions.

11 Ownership of the boat

11.1 The Boat and/or all materials and equipment purchased or appropriated from time to time by the Builders specifically for its construction (whether in their premises, upon the water or elsewhere) shall become the property of the Purchaser upon the payment of the first Stage Payment or, if later, upon the date of the said purchase or appropriation. The Builders shall however have a lien on the Boat and any materials or equipment purchased for or appropriated to the construction for recovery of all sums due (whether invoiced or not) under the terms of this Agreement or any variation or modification hereof. Any materials or equipment rejected by the Purchaser shall forthwith revest in the Builders.

11.2 The Builders shall, insofar as it is reasonably practicable to do so, mark all individual items of equipment and materials which are purchased for or appropriated to the construction of the Boat.

11.3 The Purchaser shall not without the prior written consent of the Builder which consent shall not be unreasonably withheld sell, assign, pledge or otherwise put a charge on the Boat by way of security for any indebtedness prior to delivery except for the sole purpose of obtaining a loan to finance the construction of the Boat. If the Purchaser charges the Boat in breach of the terms of this Clause, the balance of the Contract Price shall forthwith become due and payable without prejudice to any other rights or remedies of the Builders. The Purchaser shall not have the right to assign or transfer this Agreement or any of his rights and obligations hereunder without the prior written consent of the Builders.

11.4 If the Purchaser is in breach of any of the terms of this Agreement after the property in the Boat and/or materials and equipment has passed to him and the Builders wish to exercise their rights to sell the Boat and/or materials and equipment as set out herein then the property in the Boat and/or materials shall revert from the Purchaser to the Builders following 28 days' notice by the Builders of their intention to exercise such rights.

11.5 Notwithstanding the provisions of this Clause risk in the Boat shall remain with the Builders until the actual delivery of the Boat to the Purchaser.

12 Copyright

Any copyright or similar protection in manuals drawings, plans, specifications, including the Specification prepared by the Builders or their employees or agents, shall remain the property of the Builders.

13 Notices

Any notice required to be given hereunder shall be in writing and either (i) given by hand with proof of delivery or electronic transmission confirmed forthwith by first class pre-paid post, or (ii) sent by first class pre-paid post to the other party at the address set out in this Agreement or such other address in the UK as may have been notified by the other party.

14 Dispute resolution – law and jurisdiction

14.1 If during the construction of the Boat any dispute arises either as to an adjustment of the Contract Price pursuant to Clause 3.3 or as to when a Stage Payment is due and payable or as to the operation or duration of a delaying event or whether for the purposes of the policy of insurance the Boat has suffered substantial damage, then, and without prejudice to the Parties' rights to litigate such dispute, it may be referred to a single surveyor who shall be independent of the Builders and the Purchaser and whose identity and terms of reference shall be agreed by the Parties or, in default of agreement, by the President for the time being of the Yacht Designers and Surveyors Association. The surveyor so appointed shall act as an expert and not as an arbitrator and his written decision shall be final and binding upon the Parties and his fees and expenses shall be borne equally by the Parties.

14.2 This Agreement shall be construed in accordance with English law or where the Builders have their principal place of business in Scotland in accordance with Scottish law and the High Court of England or Scotland (as the case may be) shall have exclusive jurisdiction in respect of any dispute or other matter arising hereunder.

15 Interpretation

15.1 The construction of this Agreement is not to be affected by any headings.

15.2 References in this Agreement to the Parties shall include their respective successors and permitted assigns save where such succession or assignment is expressly prohibited by the terms of this Agreement.

15.3 This Agreement forms the entire agreement between the Parties and unless specifically agreed in writing by the Builders no warranty, condition, description or representation is given or to be implied by anything said or written in the negotiations between the Parties or their representatives prior to this Agreement.

15.4 If the Builders are a member of a group of companies the Builders may perform any of its obligations or exercise any of its rights hereunder by itself or through any member of its group provided that any act or omission of any such other member shall be deemed to be the act or omission of the Builders.

15.5 In this Agreement words importing the masculine gender also include the neuter and feminine gender and words importing the singular included also the plural.

15.6 Reference to any legislative provision includes a reference to that provision as amended extended or re-enacted and any replacement thereof (either before or after the date of this Agreement).

15.7 If any term or provision in this Agreement shall be held to be void in whole or in part under any enactment or rule of law such term or provision or part shall to that extent be deemed not to form part of this Agreement but the validity and enforceability of the remainder of this Agreement shall not be affected.

16 Variations and additions

This Agreement is subject to the variations and additions set out below or identified below and attached to this Agreement and initialled and dated by both Parties.

SIGNED FOR AND ON BEHALF OF THE BUILDERS

In the presence of:
Full name of witness
Address
Occupation
Signature

SIGNED FOR AND ON BEHALF OF THE PURCHASERS

In the presence of:
Full name of witness
Address
Occupation
Signature

N.B. (1 Witness in England, 2 in Scotland)

Schedule 1 – specifications

The Specification for the Boat is as set out below or as identified below and attached to this Agreement and signed by the Parties.

Schedule 2 – stage payments

Contract Price

The Boat £

Price inclusive of VAT £

   The Contract Price shall be payable by Stage Payments as set out below

1) Upon signing of this Agreement £

2) Upon the hull being available at the Builders' premises fully moulded, planked, plated or formed and confirmed in writing to the Purchaser by the Builders £

3) Upon substantial completion of the fitting of the interior joinery work or installation of the engine or stepping of the mast whichever is the earlier £

4) Upon completion of the Acceptance Trial and the signing of the Satisfaction Notice by the Purchaser or upon deemed acceptance and completion of the Builders' Certification as provided in Clauses 5.5 and 5.6 £

Schedule 3 – delivery

Delivery Date

Place of Delivery

Schedule 4 – certificate of delivery and acceptance

Place of Acceptance Trial

Date of Acceptance Trial

Persons present at Acceptance Trial:

I the undersigned hereby certify that the construction of the Boat and the Acceptance Trial have been completed to my reasonable satisfaction.
Subject to the terms of the Agreement dated [   ] this Certificate of Delivery and Acceptance will not affect my

statutory rights should the Boat or its equipment subsequently prove to be defective.
Signed by

THE PURCHASER
Dated

This form is published by the British Marine Industries Federation (BMIF) and approved by the Royal Yachting Association (RYA).

Notes

These are explanatory notes only and, although very important, do not form part of the agreement itself.

1 This form is published by the British Marine Industries Federation (BMIF) and approved by the Royal Yachting Association (RYA)

2 It is a simple form of agreement designed for the leisure marine market and cannot be expected to cater for every unforeseen circumstance arising between the parties. It is considered by the RYA and the BMIF to strike a fair balance between the interests of purchaser and the builders. Certain aspects of this agreement can be used for transactions between commercial parties.

3 It should be completed in duplicate, taking care to insert the appropriate details in clauses 1 and 2. Any specification, drawing or additional clause which cannot be accommodated on the agreement should be firmly attached to the agreement and signed by both parties. Additional clauses inserted in clause 16 should be initialled by both parties.

4 Both parties should sign (in the presence of two witnesses in Scotland).

5 The Certificate of Delivery and Acceptance must be signed by purchaser or agent on delivery and acceptance of the completed craft.

6 The first line of the contract is for the builder's use. It is recommended that the identification number should be marked on all materials and equipment intended for incorporation in the craft.

7 If it is of great importance to the purchaser that the craft should be delivered by the date specified on schedule 3, then this section should be completed.

8 **(a)** Clause 3.3 to 3.6 is a price variation clause which allows the builders to adjust the price to reflect inflation occuring between the dates of the agreement and the final installment falling due. The clause

should be deleted where the parties agree on a 'fixed-price' contract, (usually where the period between signing and final payment is likely to be short).
(b) Builders are reminded that the clause does not permit a price increase to reflect inflation occuring between original quotation and signature of the agreement. For this reason, builders should express their quotation as valid for a limited period and, if necessary, should revise it if the agreement is signed after that period.
(c) The clause allows builders to increase the price so as to reflect all increases in the Retail Price Index occurring after the date of the agreement. If they intend to rely on the clause, builders should base the price on current costs without the addition of any inflation factor.

9 If the purchaser leaves or arranges for others to leave any item on the builders' premises or on the craft, he should insure the item himself unless the builders expressly agree in writing to do so. Builders should, in any event, carry adequate insurance cover against claims arising from their negligence which result in damage to any property on their premises.

10 Statutory Rights – Nothing in this agreement shall affect the consumer's statutory rights, which rights include conformity with any description or sample, satisfactory quality and fitness for any stated purpose.

11 Copies of this agreement may be obtained from:

British Marine Industries Federation,
Marine House, Thorpe Lea Road,
Egham Surrey TW20 8BF.

or Royal Yachting Association,
RYA House, Romsey Road,
Eastleigh,
Hampshire SO50 9YA.

Agreement for the Sale of a Second-hand Yacht*

An agreement prepared by the Royal Yachting Association for the sale of a second-hand yacht between persons not normally engaged in the business of selling yachts.

AN AGREEMENT made the
day of_____ 20 ___

BETWEEN:

1 'The Vendor':

of

2 'The Purchaser'

of

The terms 'Vendor' and 'Purchaser' include their respective successors in title and the Vendor and Purchaser shall hereinafter be collectively referred to as 'the Parties'.

'The Purchase Price' : £ _____sterling

'The Deposit' : _____10% of the Purchase Price

In respect of the sale of a [REGISTERED / UNREGISTERED] PLEASURE CRAFT

Name of vessel:

Description:

Official No:

Port of Registry where applicable:

Hull Identification Number (HIN):

Now lying at:

Including all equipment, machinery and gear on board ('the Yacht') and any specific inventory attached hereto initialled by the Parties and forming part of this Agreement.

* The term 'yacht' refers to both sail and power.

1 Agreement for sale

The Vendor hereby agrees to sell and the Purchaser agrees to purchase the Yacht free from any encumbrances (subject to the conditions and terms of this agreement), together with all her outfit gear and equipment as set out in a schedule hereto but not including stores or the Vendor's personal effects, for the Purchase Price.

2 Payment of deposit

On the signing of this agreement the Deposit is to be paid to the Vendor and the balance of the Purchase Price together with any Value Added Tax shall be payable in accordance with Clause 6.

3.1 Value Added Tax

The Vendor [is/is not] a registered person for the purpose of the regulations relating to Value Added Tax and the Purchase Price [is/is not] exclusive of Value Added Tax.

3.2 Import dues and local taxes (craft lying overseas)

The Vendor warrants that the craft has been properly imported into [   ] and that all appropriate local taxes and dues have been paid and that the proposed sale is in accordance with all relevant local laws and regulations.

4 Inspection survey

The Purchaser may, at a venue to be agreed and at his own cost, haul out or place ashore/or open up the Yacht and her machinery for the purposes of inspection and/or survey which, including any written report, shall be completed within [   ] days of the signing of this agreement. If any inspection requires more than superficial non-destructive dismantling the consent of the Vendor must be obtained before such work commences.

5.1 Notice of defects

Within fourteen days after completion of such inspection and/or survey if any material defect(s) in the Yacht or her machinery other than disclosed to the Purchaser in writing prior to the signing of this agreement or any material deficiencies in her inventory, if any, shall have been found the Purchaser may either:

5.1.1 give notice to the Vendor of his rejection of the Yacht provided that the notice shall specify any material defect(s) or deficiencies; or

5.1.2 give notice to the Vendor specifying any material defect(s) or deficiencies and requiring the Vendor forthwith either to make good the same or make a sufficient reduction in the Purchase Price to enable the Purchaser to make good the same. All agreed items of work to be completed without undue delay in all circumstances and to be carried out so as to satisfy the expressly specified requirements of the Purchaser's surveyor in respect only of material defects mentioned in his report and specified in the notice to the Vendor.

5.2 If the Purchaser shall have served a notice of rejection under Clause 5.1.1, then this agreement shall be deemed to be rescinded forthwith and the Vendor shall refund to the purchaser the Deposit in accordance with Clause 8.

5.3 If the Purchaser shall have served a notice under Clause 5.1.2 requiring the Vendor to make good material defects or deficiencies or to make a reduction in the Purchase Price, and the Vendor shall not have agreed within twenty one days after the service of the notice to make good such defects or the Parties have not agreed in the twenty one days after the service of notice upon the reduction in the Purchase Price, then this agreement shall be deemed to have been rescinded on the twenty second day after the service of notice and the Vendor shall refund to the Purchaser the Deposit in accordance with Clause 8.

In the case of any deficiencies in the Yacht's inventory (if any) remaining or arising within seven days of acceptance in accordance with Clause 6 the deficiencies shall be made good or a reduction in the Purchase Price shall be agreed, failing which this agreement shall be rescinded at the option of the Purchaser only.

6.1 Acceptance of yacht

The Yacht shall be deemed to have been accepted by the Purchaser and the balance of the Purchase Price and any Value Added Tax thereon shall become due and payable in accordance with Clause 7 upon the happening of any of the following events:

6.2 The expiry of fourteen days from the date of this agreement or such extended period as may be agreed between the Parties provided that no inspection or survey has been commenced;

6.3 The expiry of fifteen days from the completion of the survey, provided that the Purchaser has not served notice under Clause 5.1;

6.4 Notification in writing by the Vendor to the Purchaser of completion of the remedial works specified in a notice given by the Purchaser under Clause 5.1.2;

7.1 Completion of sale

Upon acceptance of the Yacht by the Purchaser, the Deposit shall be treated as part payment of the Purchase Price. Within seven days of acceptance the Purchaser shall pay the balance of the Purchase Price and any Value Added Tax thereon and the Vendor shall:

In the case of a registered yacht:
7.1.1 *Registered yacht*
  provide the Purchaser with the Certificate of Registry, correct and

updated, together with any other documents appertaining to the Yacht and shall execute a Bill of Sale, in the prescribed form, in favour of the Purchaser or his nominee, showing the Yacht to be free from encumbrances and completed so as to ensure transfer on the Register;

OR
7.1.2 *In the case of an unregistered yacht (including a yacht registered on the SSR)*
  (a) Provide the Purchaser with a Bill of Sale in favour of the Purchaser or his nominee, together with any other documents appertaining to the Yacht;
  (b) Deliver to the Purchaser any necessary delivery order or other authority enabling the Purchaser to take immediate possession of the Yacht.

7.2 Where payment is made by cheque, draft, letter of credit or other instrument, the terms of this agreement shall not be deemed to have been fulfilled until such payment is cleared into the payee's account.

7.3 Vendor's right to assign title

By delivery of the documents specified in either case the Vendor shall be deemed to have covenanted AND HEREBY COVENANTS that he has the right to transfer property in the Yacht and that the same is free from all encumbrances, debts, liens and the like except such encumbrances and liabilities for duties, taxes, debts, liens and the like as are the responsibility of the Purchaser under Clauses 4 and 8.

7.4 Free access after completion

On completion, the Vendor shall ensure that the Yacht is available for collection by the Purchaser and that free access by the Purchaser together with all necessary haulage equipment is permitted at no additional cost to the Purchaser.

8.1 Rescission of agreement

In the event of rescission of this agreement by the Purchaser he shall, at his own expense, reinstate the Yacht to the condition and position in which he found her, and shall pay all boatyard and surveyor's charges for this work.

8.2 Return of deposit

The Vendor shall thereupon return the Deposit to the Purchaser without deduction and without interest save that he shall be entitled to retain such part of the Deposit as shall be necessary to defray any boatyard or surveyor's charges not paid by the Purchaser.

Neither party shall thereafter have any claim against the other under this agreement.

9 Warranties

The Vendor being a person not selling the Yacht in the course of a business, and the Purchaser being at liberty to inspect the Yacht and satisfy himself as to her condition and specification, all express or implied warranties or conditions, statutory or otherwise, are hereby excluded and the Yacht, her outfit, gear and equipment shall be taken with all defects and faults of description without any allowance or abatement whatsoever.

10 Risk

Until the Yacht has been accepted or shall be deemed to have been accepted by the Purchaser she shall be at the risk of the Vendor who shall make good all damage sustained by her before the date of acceptance. If the Yacht be lost or becomes a constructive total loss before such acceptance, this agreement shall be null and void except that the Purchaser will be liable for the cost of all work authorised by him under Clauses 4 and 8 and undertaken before such loss took place and the Deposit shall be returned to the Purchaser without interest but less any deduction made under Clauses 4 and 8 and otherwise without

deduction and the Purchaser shall have no claim against the Vendor for damages or otherwise. After acceptance the Yacht shall in all respects be at the risk of the Purchaser.

Notwithstanding the provisions of this clause the ownership of the Yacht will not vest in the Purchaser until payment of the balance of the Purchase Price in accordance with Clause 7 even though the Purchaser may have insured his risk under the provisions of this clause.

11.1 Default by Purchaser

Should the Purchaser fail to pay the balance of the Purchase Price in accordance with Clause 7, the Vendor may give notice in writing to the Purchaser requiring him to complete the purchase within fourteen days of the service of such notice.

If the Purchaser fails to comply with the notice then the Vendor may re-sell the Yacht by public auction or private treaty and any deposit paid shall thereupon be forfeit without prejudice to the Vendor's right to claim from the Purchaser the amount of any loss on re-sale together with all his reasonable costs and expenses, due allowance being made for any forfeited deposit. On the expiry of the said notice the Yacht shall be at the Vendor's risk.

11.2 Default by Vendor

If the Vendor shall default in the execution of his part of the contract the Purchaser shall, without prejudice to any other rights he may have hereunder, be entitled to the return of the Deposit.

Unless such default by the Vendor shall have arisen from events over which the Vendor had no control, the Vendor shall pay interest upon the amount of the Deposit for the period during which he has held it at the rate of 4% per annum above finance house base rate, together with compensation for any loss which the Purchaser may have sustained as a result of the Vendor's default.

12 Arbitration

All disputes that cannot be resolved between the Parties and which arise out of or in connection with this agreement shall be submitted to a single arbitrator to be appointed, in default of agreement, by the Chairman of the Council of the RYA and the provisions of the Arbitration Act shall apply.

13 Notices

Any notice under this agreement shall be in writing and any notice to the Purchaser or Vendor shall be sufficiently served if delivered to him personally or posted by recorded delivery to his last known address. Any notice posted shall be deemed to have been received forty eight hours after the time of posting and any notice given in any other manner shall be deemed to have been received at the time when, in the ordinary course of post, it may be expected to have been received.

14 Jurisdiction

This agreement shall be construed according to, and governed by the Law of England (or of Scotland if the Vendor's address shall be in that country) and the Parties hereby submit to the jurisdiction of the Courts of the same countries.

15 Marginal notes

The construction of this agreement is not to be affected by any marginal notes.

16 Rights under contract or statute

This agreement forms the entire agreement between the Parties unless otherwise specifically agreed in writing between them.

SIGNED BY THE VENDOR

In the presence of:

SIGNED BY THE PURCHASER

In the presence of:

British Marine Industries Federation Code of Practice for the Sale of Used Boats

Broker and vendor/purchaser

1 Legal liability to disclose information

(i) *Vendors*

Brokers must incorporate into 'instructions to sell' forms and/or particulars/questionnaire forms, a clause to the effect:

'The Vendor declares that to the best of his knowledge and belief the particulars given to the Broker and signed or supplied by the Vendor are correct, and that he has power to dispose of the vessel with the concurrence of any joint owner or mortgagee or hire purchase company and all known defects have been declared and that he understands the implications of the Misrepresentations Act of 1976 and agrees to indemnify the Broker against all costs, claims and demands arising in consequence of any of the information given in the particulars being incorrect.'

(ii) *Brokers*

The Broker is responsible for providing accurate information to the best of his ability, and defects or deficiencies in a boat of which the Broker is aware must be divulged to Purchasers and the Vendor.

2 Central Agencies (Sole Agents)

Central Agency instructions from Vendors must be in writing and must be produced by the Central Agent on request of another Member. If a Vendor states his intention of appointing only one agent, but reserves the right to sell his boat privately, this is not a Central Agency.

3 Offers

In the absence of express agreement to the contrary, the Vendor's approval to sell must be obtained even when the asking price has been offered and all offers must be submitted until such time as a deposit acceptable to the Vendor is paid and the terms agreed by the Vendor.

4 Contract

An Agreement for the Sale and Purchase of a second-hand yacht on a recognised ABYA approved form should always be used, but, in the absence of such an agreement, it is recommended that Brokers establish a contract in the form of a receipt or otherwise by memorandum. Such receipt or memorandum should state that any deposit paid is deemed to be held on the terms of the said ABYA approved form.

5 Quoted prices

Brokers must not offer boats at a lower figure than that quoted by the Vendor. The price quoted shall be in all cases the gross price inclusive of commission. Where applicable, any VAT liability must be indicated in accordance with current legislation.

6 Surveys

Other than in exceptional circumstances, a Broker should always advise a Purchaser to have a survey. However, a Broker should not recommend a particular surveyor but may accept the Purchaser's instructions to appoint a surveyor on his behalf. On no account shall the Broker make or receive a commission in connection with the survey.

7 Sale proceeds

The Broker shall be responsible for keeping the deposit, part payments and the proceeds of the sale in a separate banking account designated for the purpose, and shall account for the same to the Vendor after deducting such commission as may be properly due to the Broker or his Sharing Broker within fourteen days of the sale being effected, or where applicable after transfer of clear title to the Purchaser, whichever shall be later.

8 Title and registration

At the time of the sale the Lead Broker shall obtain evidence of title a properly executed Bill of Sale or receipt showing the boat to be free from encumbrances, which shall be exchanged for the cleared purchase monies for the boat. Brokers are required to provide the facility, at a reasonable extra charge, to their clients for dealing with British Registration procedures and Customs Documentation.

(Practice Note: While a Purchaser or Vendor is not obliged to engage a Broker to transfer ownership of a registered vessel, the Broker is strongly advised to encourage the Purchaser and Vendor to appoint him for this purpose, and it is recommended that only modest fees be charged for this service on order to encourage continuity of Registration.)

9 Standard disclaimer for particulars

It is recommended that the following wording is included in any particulars shown to a prospective purchaser.

'In this case we are acting as Brokers only. The Vendor is/is not selling in the course of business. [Delete as necessary.]

Whilst every care has been taken in their preparation, the correctness of these particulars is not guaranteed. The particulars are intended only as a guide and they do not constitute a term of any contract. A prospective buyer is strongly advised to check the particulars and where appropriate, at his own expense to employ a qualified marine surveyor to carry out a survey and/or to have an engine trial conducted.'

(Practice Note: This disclaimer will not be appropriate in all circumstances and care should be taken to ensure that it is suitably amended and/or deleted as necessary, for example; in the case where the Broker is acting as a principal; where the Vendor is selling in the course of business; where VAT is payable; if an engine is not fitted and so on.)

Appendix 4

RYA Bill of Sale for Private Transactions

A simple Bill of Sale for use between a private buyer and a private seller of a motor cruiser not on the Part I Register of British Ships

BILL OF SALE

FOR THE MOTOR CRUISER
Type:
Year built:
Length:
Beam:
Power:
Small Ships Register No: ('the Motor Cruiser')

I/We

....   [and ....
of: ....   of ....
....
                                                                        ('the Transferor[s]')

IN CONSIDERATION of the sum of   £ ....
(..   pounds) paid to me/us
by..   [and ....
of: ....   of ....
....
                                                                        ('the Transferee[s]')

receipt of which is acknowledged
1.   transfer the Yacht to the Transferee[s];
2.   for myself/ourselves and for my/our heirs covenant with the Transferees and
            his/their heirs and assigns that I/we have power so to transfer and that the
            yacht is free from encumbrances.

SIGNED this............................   day of ....   20[   ]
.... (signature of Transferor[s]
[..]

in the presence of:
....(signature of witness)
....(signature of witness)
....(signature of witness)

Notes: 1. This form of the bill of Sale is produced by the RYA for use by personal members on the transfer of an unregistered yacht or a yacht registered on the Small Ships Register. Transfers of yachts registered under Part I of the Register of British Ships should be evidenced using the form approved by the Registry of Shipping and Seamen, PO Box 165, Cardiff CF4 5FU.
2. Please delete inapplicable alternatives.
3. This form of Bill of Sale should not be used if any of the parties to it is a corporate body.

VAT Guide for Yachts

issued by HM Customs and Excise

(*Not including Channel Islands, Malta or Gibraltar*)

This leaflet is for UK yachtsmen who still have concerns about VAT when cruising in the EC or when returning from outside the EC.

VESSELS PURCHASED/ACQUIRED WITHIN THE EC

UK residents should only use a boat in the Community if it is VAT paid, or 'deemed' VAT paid. Documentary evidence supporting this should be carried at all times.

- Original invoice or receipt
- Evidence that VAT was paid at importation

If the vessel was in use as a private pleasure craft before 1/1/1985 *and* was in the EC on 31/12/1992, it may be 'deemed' VAT paid under an age-related relief. Documentary evidence to support this could be:

For Age
- Marine survey
- Part 1 Registration
- Insurance documents
- Builders certificate

For Location at 31/12/92
- Receipt for mooring
- Receipt for harbour dues
- Dry dock records

As Austria, Finland and Sweden joined the Single Market two years later, the relevant dates will be .... in use before 1/1/1987 and moored in EC on 31/12/1994.
    Other documents which could demonstrate VAT status could be:

- Evidence that Returned Goods Relief (RGR) has been granted
- Evidence that Transfer of Residence Relief (TOR) has been granted (Subject to one year restriction on disposal).

In the absence of any of the above, whilst cruising within the EC you should carry a Bill of Sale (between two private individuals in the UK). Whilst this is not conclusive proof that VAT has been paid, it does indicate that tax status is the responsibility of UK Customs.

VESSELS PURCHASED/ACQUIRED OUTSIDE THE EC

ANY yacht purchased outside the EC will be liable for VAT, regardless of age or previous tax history. There may also be Import Duty unless the vessel is more than 12m overall or built in the EC. Charges become due at the first port of call within the EC (See Public Notice No 3).

BUYING A NEW VESSEL IN ONE MEMBER STATE OF THE EC TO TAKE TO ANOTHER

Yachts purchased NEW within the EC pay VAT at the country of destination. For example, if you buy a new yacht in France, you should send appendix D of Public Notice No 728 to the local Customs and Excise office within 7 days of arrival in the UK.

BUYING A VESSEL IN THE UK FOR EXPORT FROM THE EC

You can purchase a vessel tax free if you intend to export it, under its own power to a destination outside the EC. Full details can be found in VAT leaflet 703/3/98.

VOYAGES OUTSIDE THE EC

Part 1 of form C1331 should be lodged with Customs prior to departure if you are going directly to a country outside the EC, ie Channel Islands, Malta and Gibraltar etc. On return to the UK you should report your arrival as per Public Notice No. 8 page 6.

For further information contact your local Advice Centre, or look in your phone book under Customs and Excise.

This information sheet is produced by the National Unit for Personal Transport (PTU) HM Customs and Excise (MSO), PO Box 242, Dover CT17 9GP.

Appendix 6

EU Recreational Craft Directive

Importing of a second-hand boat into the European Economic Area (EEA) and boats built for own use

General
Since 16 June 1998 all recreational craft, with few exceptions, between 2.5m and 24m in length, imported into the European Economic Area for the first time, and home-built boats if placed on the market within five years of completion, must comply with the essential requirements of the RCD and must be CE marked to certify this compliance. The builder, his agent or the person importing the boat is responsible for such compliance and marking.

Application
The European Economic Area (EEA) includes all EU countries and their dependent territories plus Iceland and Norway.
Put into service means the first use by the end user but does not include boats temporarily put into service for reasons of tourism or transit.
Placing on the market means the first making available against payment or free of charge.

Boats that will need to comply with the Directive and be CE marked
These include:
* Boats built outside the EEA which were not put into service in the EEA prior to 16 June 1998.
* Boats built for own use if subsequently placed on the EEA market during a period of five years of completion.

Boats that will not need to comply with the Directive
These include:
- Boats completed or put into service in the EEA prior to 16 June 1998.
- Boats built in the EEA prior to 16 June 1998 even if exported and subsequently re-imported after 16 June 1998.
- Boats built for own use provided they are not subsequently placed on the EEA market during a period of five years.
- Boats intended for racing and labelled as such by the manufacturer, his agent or the importer.
- Canoes, kayaks, gondolas, pedalos, sailing surfboards, powered surfboards and personal watercraft.
- Boats designed before 1950, built predominantly of the original materials and labelled as such by the manufacturer, his agent or the importer.
- All boats entering the EEA for reasons of tourism or in transit.

Should you be in any doubt whatsoever about whether or not your boat needs to comply then contact the RYA.
You should consider this carefully as should your boat need to comply and you fail to ensure this you may be subject to three months' imprisonment and/or £5,000 fine.

Compliance with the Directive
Should your boat need to comply with the Directive the RYA can help by supplying a 'RYA RCD Post Construction Compliance Pack' which may be used as a guide for correct compliance. To obtain this pack contact the RYA Technical Unit.

A Guide to Publications available from the RYA of Particular Interest to Motor Boaters

Books	RYA Reference
Day Skipper Shorebased Notes	DSN
Motor Cruising Practical Course Notes	MCP
Sea Survival Practical Notes	SSPCN
Collision Regulations	G2/90
Marina Guide	G8/2000
Cruising Yacht Safety (Sail & Power)	C8/98
Motor Cruising Log Book	G18/98
Power Boat Log Book	G20/96
Buying a New Yacht	G10/2000
Buying a Second-Hand Yacht	G21/2000
VHF Radio SRC Assessments	G26/2000
RYA Book of Navigation	BN
RYA Book of Navigation Exercises	ZN03
The Macmillan Reeds Nautical Almanac	ZM22
Inshore Navigation	Z101
Boat Owner's Highway Code	ZB04
Motor Boating	ZM14
The Seaman's Guide to Rule of the Road	SGR
The RYA Book of Euro Regs	ZE02
The RYA Book of Diesel Engines	ZD01
The RYA Book of Outboard Engines	Z003
Where to Launch Around the Coast	ZW12

Videos	
First Aid Afloat	DV4
Life on the Line	CV11
Marine Diesel Engines	CV12
Boat Handling	CV41

Appendix 8

RYA National Cruising Scheme – Motor Cruising Courses

Course	Minimum experience	Assumed knowledge	Course content	Ability after course	Minimum duration
Introduction to Motor Cruising	None	None	Boating safety and basic seamanship	Useful crew member in motor cruiser	
Helmsman's course	Some practical experience desirable	None	Boating safety, helmsmanship, handling, introduction to engine maintenance	Competent to handle a motor cruiser of specific type in sheltered waters	2 days
Day Skipper Shorebased	Some practical experience desirable	None	Basic seamanship, and introduction to navigation and meteorology		
Day Skipper Practical	Basic navigation and helmsmanship	Pilotage, boat handling, seamanship and navigation	Skipper a motor cruiser in familiar waters by day		4 days
Diesel engine course	None	None	Diesel engine operation, maintenance and simple defect rectification	Operate a diesel engine effectively and carry out simple repairs	6 hours
Coastal Skipper Yachtmaster Shorebased	None	Navigation to Day Skipper shorebased standard	Offshore and coastal navigation, pilotage, meteorology		
Coastal Skipper /Yachtmaster Practical	15 days (2 as skipper); 300 miles; 8 night hours	Navigation to Coastal Skipper shorebased standard Boat handling to Day Skipper practical standard	Skippering techniques for coastal and offshore passages	Skipper a yacht on coastal passages by day and night	5 days
Yachtmaster Ocean Shorebased	Coastal and offshore passages	Navigation to Coastal Skipper and Yachtmaster	Astro navigation ocean meteorology, passage planning offshore standard		

Full details of the RYA Motor Cruising Course Syllabi can be found in RYA publication ref. G18/98 available direct from the RYA or from many yacht chandleries.

In an effort to give you a flavour of the requirements of the RYA courses ideal for those buying their first motor cruiser, I have included the syllabi of the Day Skipper Shorebased and Tidal Practical courses and the RYA Diesel Engine course, all of which I would highly recommend, preferably *before* setting out for the first time or alternatively soon thereafter.

RYA/DoT Certificates of Competence

Grade of examination	Minimum sea time (within 10 yrs of exam)	Form of examination	Certificates required before examination
RYA National Motor Cruising Certificate	100 days 200 miles at sea 6 night hours	None Award on request	Day Skipper shorebased and practical course completion certificates
RYA/DoT Coastal Skipper	30 days 2 days as skipper 800 miles 12 night hours	Practical	Restricted (VHF only) Radio Operator's Certificate First Aid Certificate
RYA/DoT Yachtmaster Offshore	50 days 5 days as skipper 2,500 miles 5 passages over 60 miles, including 2 overnight and 2 as skipper	Practical	Restricted (VHF only) Radio Operator's Certificate First Aid Certificate
RYA/DoT Yachtmaster Ocean	Ocean passage as skipper or mate of watch	Oral and assessment of sights taken at sea. (Written exam in lieu of shorebased course completion certificate)	RYA/DoT Yachtmaster Offshore Certificate Yachtmaster Ocean shore-based course completion certificate

DAY SKIPPER
Shorebased Syllabus

Subject	Broad detail to be covered	Minimum time (in hours)	Depth of knowledge
1 Nautical terms	1 Parts of a boat and hull 2 General nautical terminology	2	B
2 Rope work	1 Knowledge of the properties of synthetic ropes in common use 2 Ability to make, and knowledge of the use of: figure of eight, bowline, clove hitch, reef knot, single and double sheet bend, rolling hitch, round turn and two half hitches 3 Securing to cleats, use of winches and general rope handling	3	B B C
3 Anchor work	1 Characteristics of different types of anchor 2 Considerations to be taken into account when anchoring	1	B B
4 Safety	1 Knowledge of the safety equipment to be carried, its stowage and use (RYA booklet C8) 2 Fire precautions and fire fighting 3 Use of personal safety equipment, harnesses and lifejackets 4 Ability to send a distress signal by VHF radiotelephone 5 Basic knowledge of rescue procedures including helicopter rescue	3	B B B B B
5 International Regulations for Preventing Collisions at Sea	1 Steering and sailing rules (5,7,8,9,10 and 12-19) 2 General rules (all other rules)	2	A B
6 Definition of position, course and speed	1 Latitude and longitude 2 Knowledge of standard navigational terms 3 True bearings and courses 4 The knot	1	B B B C
7 Navigational charts and publications	1 Information shown on charts, chart symbols and representation of direction and distance 2 Navigational publications in common use 3 Chart correction	2	B C C
8 Navigational drawing instruments	1 Use of parallel rulers, dividers and proprietary plotting instruments	1	B

Subject	Broad detail to be covered	Minimum time (in hours)	Depth of knowledge
9 Compasses	1 Application of variation 2 Use of transits and comparison to check deviation 3 Importance of swinging compass 4 Use of hand bearing compass 5 Siting of steering compass	3	B B B C
10 Chart work	1 Working up position from course steered, distance run and estimates of leeway and set 2 Plotting fixes 3 Working out course to steer to allow for leeway and set	5	B B B
11 Position fixing	1 Sources of position lines 2 Potential accuracy of fixing methods 3 GPS	2	B C B
12 Tides and tidal streams	1 Tidal definitions, levels and datum 2 Tide tables, standard and secondary ports 3 Use of Admiralty method of determining tidal height at standard port 4 Use of tidal diamonds and tidal stream atlases for chart work	4	B C B B
13 Visual aids to navigation	1 Lighthouses and beacons, light characteristics	1	B
14 Meteorology	1 Sources of broadcast meteorological information 2 Knowledge of terms used in shipping forecasts, including the Beaufort scale, and their significance to small craft 3 Basic knowledge of highs, lows, and fronts	3	B B C
15 Passage planning	1 Preparation of navigational plan for short coastal passages 2 Meteorological considerations in planning short coastal passages	2	C B
16 Navigation in restricted visibility	1 Precautions to be taken and limitations imposed by fog	1	B
17 Pilotage	1 Use of transits, leading lines and clearing lines 2 IALA system of buoyage for Region A 3 Use of sailing directions 4 Pilotage plans and harbour entry	3	B B B B
18 Responsibility for avoiding pollution and protecting the marine environment		1	B

Key: *Guide to Depths of Knowledge:* A = Full knowledge, B = Working knowledge, C = Outline knowledge

DAY SKIPPER (Tidal)
Practical Syllabus

1 Preparation for sea

Able to prepare a motor cruiser for sea, carry out fuel and engine checks, secure and stow gear above and below decks.

2 Boat handling

Able to carry out the following manoeuvres under power in various wind and tide conditions. Is aware of considerations which arise in boats with different hull forms and propeller configurations.

- Steering a straight course
- Turning in a confined space
- Anchoring at a pre-determined position
- Berthing alongside
- Leaving an alongside berth
- Picking up a mooring buoy
- Berthing between piles or head and stern buoys
- Recovery of man overboard
- Understanding the principles of power trim and trim tabs and their correct use

3 Navigation

Is proficient in chart work and can carry out the following tasks:

- Taking and plotting fixes
- Working up a dead reckoning (DR) and estimated position (EP)
- Predicting tidal heights and tidal streams
- Working out course to steer to allow for tidal stream
- Identifying buoys and lights by colour, shape, top mark and light characteristics
- Keeping a navigational log
- Using an echo sounder
- Use of GPS

4 Passage making

Able to plan and make a coastal passage taking into account the type of boat and the strengths of the crew.

5 Pilotage

Can prepare and execute a pilotage plan for entry into or departure from harbour.

Understands the use of leading and clearing lines, transits and soundings as aids to pilotage.

6 Meteorology

Knows sources of forecast information, can interpret forecasts and is able to use a barometer as a forecasting aid.

7 Rules of the road

Has a working knowledge of the application of the International Regulations for Preventing Collisions at Sea.

8 Use of engines

Has a knowledge of the prevention of common engine faults and is competent in the following areas:

- Checks before starting, during running and after stopping
- Periodic maintenance checks on engines and electrical installations
- Requirements for tool kits, spares and lubricants
- Fuel consumption at different speeds
- Knows how to clean water filters and raw water pump impellers
- Knows how to bleed fuel systems and change fuel filters
- Knows how to change transmission belts of pumps and alternators

9 Emergency situations

Knows correct action to take in emergency situations, including:

- Fire
- Hull damage
- Medical emergency
- Towing and being towed
- VHF emergency procedures
- Helicopter rescue

10 Night cruising

Has experienced motor cruising at night, including leaving and entering harbour, and understands special considerations for keeping a lookout and identifying marks by night.

RYA Diesel Engine Course Syllabus

Aim of Course

To give an awareness of the main systems of a marine diesel engine so that the yachtsman can take simple measures to prevent mechanical breakdown at sea and rectify defects which do not require workshop support. No pre-course knowledge is required.

1 Introduction

Principles of the diesel engine

2 The four stroke cycle

- Naturally aspirated engines
- Turbocharging
- Intercooling/aftercooling

3 The fuel system

- The basic system
- The tank
- The water separating pre-filter
- Fuel lift pump
- The engine fine filter
- Injection pump
- Injectors
- Bleeding the system

4 The cooling system

- Seawater cooling
- Freshwater cooling
- Temperature control

- The thermostat
- The seawater impeller pump

5 The air systems

- The airway in
- The airway out

6 Engine electrical systems

- The basic system
- Battery capacity and care
- Drive belts
- The alternator

7 Spares and tool requirements

- Basic spares and tools

8 Importance of winterisation and servicing

- Engine lubrication
- Transmission lubrication
- Winterisation and servicing
- Service schedule
- Winterisation

9 Fault-finding

Course Requirements

The minimum duration of the course is six hours. A diesel engine (not necessarily in working condition) will be provided for practical sessions. (No more than six students to one engine.) Instructors will have attended an RYA Training Course.

Enquiries to: RYA,
RYA House, Romsey Road, Eastleigh,
Hampshire SO50 9YA.
Tel: 02380 627400
Fax: 02380 629924

Useful Addresses and Contact Details

American Bureau of Shipping
(Classification Society)
ABS House
1 Frying Pan Alley
London El 7HS
Tel: 020 7247 3255
Fax: 020 7377 2453
E-mail: abs@eagle.org
Website: www.eagle.org

Association of Brokers & Yacht Agents
(& Classification Society)
The Wheel House
Petersfield Road
Whitehill, Bordon
Hampshire GU35 9BU
Tel: 01420 473862
Fax: 01420 488328
E-mail: info@ybdsa.co.uk

Boatmark Ltd.
(Boatmark Registration Scheme)
Dolphin House
PO Box 61, New Street
Salisbury
Wiltshire SP1 2TB
Tel: 01722 413346
Fax: 01722 412746
E-mail: bmif@bmif.co.uk
Website:
www.bigblue.org.uk/html/Boatmark.cfm

British Marine Industries Federation
Meadlake Place
Thorpe Lea Road
Egham
Surrey TW20 8HE
Tel: 01784 473377
Fax: 01784 439 678
E-mail: bmif@bmif.co.uk
Website: www.bmif.co.uk

Bureau Veritas (Classification Society)
Capital House
42 Weston Street
London SE1 3QL
Tel: 020 7403 6266
Fax: 020 7403 1590
E-mail: info@bvqi.com
Website: www.bvqi.com

Det Norske Veritas (Classification Society)
Palace House
3 Cathedral Street
London SE1 9DE
Tel: 020 7357 6080
Fax: 020 7357 6048
E-mail: london.ship@dnv.com
Website: www.dnv.com

Germanischer Lloyd (Classification Society)
Elmcourt
53 Elmcroft Road
Orpington BR6 0HZ
Tel: 01689 891911
Fax: 01689 891876
E-mail: gl-london@germanlloyd.org
Website: www.germanlloyd.org

Institute of Marine Engineers
The Memorial Building
76 Mark Lane
London EC3R 7JN
Tel: 020 7382 2600
Fax: 020 7382 2670
E-mail: imare@imare.org.uk
Website: www.imare.org.uk

Lloyds Register of Shipping Yacht & Small Craft Services
(Classification Society)
100 Leadenhall Street
London EC3A 3BP
Tel: 020 7709 9166
Fax: 020 7488 4796
E-mail: it.helpdesk@lr.org
Website: www.lr.org

Radiocommunications Agency
Aeronautical and Maritime Section
Wyndham House
189 Marsh Wall
London E14 9SX
Tel: 020 7211 0215
Fax: 020 7211 0228
E-mail: ams@ra.gtnet.gov.uk
Website: www.radio.gov.uk

Registrar General of Shipping and Seamen
(for Part I Registration)
PO Box 165
Cardiff CF4 5FU
Tel: 029 2074 7333
Fax: 029 2074 7877
E-mail: rss@mcga.gov.uk
Website: www.mcagency.org.uk

Registro Italiano Navale
(Classification Society)
l4 Waterloo Place
London SWIY 4AR
Tel: 020 7839 6099
Fax: 020 7930 2950
E-mail: london.office@rina.org
Website: www.rina.org

Royal Institute of Naval Architects
9 Upper Belgrave Street
London SW1X 8BQ
Tel: 020 7235 4622
Fax: 020 7259 5912
E-mail: hq@rina.org.uk
Website: www.rina.org.uk

Royal Yachting Association
(& Classification Society)
RYA House,
Romsey Road
Eastleigh
Hampshire S050 9YA
Tel: 023 8062 7400
Fax: 023 8062 9924
E-mail: admin@rya.org.uk
Website: www.rya.org.uk

Small Ships Register
(for Part III Registration (SSR))
PO Box 508
Cardiff CF4 5FH
Tel: 029 2074 7333
Fax: 029 2074 7877
E-mail: rss@mcga.gov.uk
Website: www.mcagency.org.uk

The Radio Licensing Centre
Post Office Customer Management
PO Box 1495
Bristol BS99 3QS

Yacht Designers and Surveyors Association
(& Classification Society)
Wheel House,
Petersfield Road
Whitehill
Bordon
Hampshire GU35 9BU
Tel: 01420 473862
Fax: 01420 488328
E-mail: info@ybdsa.co.uk

A selection of RYA sea schools specialising in motor cruiser training

(The complete list can be obtained from the RYA Training Department 023 8062 7400)

Capital Training
Mewstone Cottage
Back Lane
Sway
Hants SO41 6BU
Tel: 01590 683496
Fax: 01590 681232
E-mail: capital-training@intonet.co.uk
Website: www.capital-training.co.uk

Dover Sea School
12 Vale Square
Ramsgate
Kent CT11 9BX
Tel: 01843 852858
Fax: 01843 852772
E-mail: Michael.oram@btinternet.com
Website: www.doverseaschool.co.uk

East Anglian Sea School
Suffolk Yacht Harbour
Levington
Near Ipswich
Suffolk IP10 0LN
Tel: 01473 659992
Fax: 01473 659994
E-mail: eassltd@aol.com
Website: www.members.aol.com/eassltd

Medway Cruising School
Manor Lane
Borstal
Rochester
Kent ME1 3HS
Tel: 01634 844664
Fax: 01634 844664
E-mail: info@medwaycruisingschool.com
Website: www.medwaycruisingschool.com

National Federation of Sea Schools
(RYA Sea Schools Association)
159 Woodlands Road
Woodlands
Southampton SO40 7GL
Tel: 023 8029 3822
Fax: 023 8029 3822
E-mail: kay@nfss.co.uk
Website: www.nfss.co.uk

Peters Sea Tech
Chichester Marina
Chichester
West Sussex PO20 7EJ
Tel: 01243 511381
Fax: 01243 511382
E-mail: sales@petersplc.com
Website: www.petersplc.com

RAMAR Sea Training
Robert Avis
PO Box 2000
Kenley CR8 5XL
Tel: 020 8660 6643
Fax: 020 8660 1330
E-mail: enquiries@ramar-international.co.uk
Website: www.ramar-international.co.uk

Southern Professional Training
305 Swanwick Lane
Swanwick
Southampton SO31 7GT
Tel: 01489 575511
Fax: 01489 578828
E-mail: sailing@southern.co.uk
Website: www.southern.co.uk

Yacht finance

Bank of Scotland
Freepost LS69
Alleyn House
23/27 Carlton Crescent
Southampton SO15 2RB
Tel: 023 8033 3467
Fax: 023 8063 1514

Lombard Marine Finance
Lombard North Central PLC
371 Millbrook Road West
Southampton SO15 0HW
Tel: 023 8051 5050
Fax: 023 8051 5070
E-mail: marine@lombard.co.uk
Website: www.lombard.co.uk/marine

Mercantile Credit Marine Finance
Saltmakers House
Hamble Point Marina
School Lane, Hamble
Southampton SO31 4NB
Tel: 0800 445644
Fax: 023 8045 6302
E-mail: hamble.office@barclays.co.uk
Website: www.mercantile-credit.co.uk

Yacht insurance

Bishop Skinner & Co Ltd
(Insurance Brokers)
5 Oakley Crescent
City Road
London EC1V 1NU
Tel: 0800 783 8057
Fax: 020 7608 2171
E-mail: insurance@bishopskinner.com
Website: www.bishopskinner.com

GJW Direct
Silkhouse Court
Tithebarn Street
Liverpool L2 2QW
Tel: 0500 141141

Fax: 0151 236 0761
E-mail: paul.clarke@cox.co.uk

Navigators & General Insurance Company Ltd
PO Box 848
Brighton BN1 4PR
Tel: 01273 863420
Fax: 01273 863401
E-mail: enquiries@navigatorsandgeneral.co.uk

Pantaenius Yacht Insurance
Marine Building
Victoria Wharf
Plymouth PL4 0RF
Tel: 01752 223656
Fax: 01752 223637
E-mail: info@pantaenius.co.uk
Website: www.pantaenius.co.uk

St Margaret's Insurances Ltd
153-155 High Street
London SE20 7DL
Tel: 0800 0180012
Fax: 020 8659 1968
E-mail: yachts@stminsurance.co.uk
Website: www.stminsurance.co.uk

WG Insurance
PO Box 3000
Coulsdon CR5 3ZP
Tel: 01737 557020
Fax: 01737 556877
E-mail: wgyachts@lineone.net
Website: www.yachtinsurance.org.uk

Useful motor cruising magazines

Boat International
Ward House
5-7 Kingston Hill
Kingston-upon-Thames
Surrey KT2 2PW
Tel: 020 8547 2662
Fax: 020 8547 1201
Website: www.boatinternational.com

Boat Mart International
First Floor
Edward House
Tindal Bridge
Edward Street
Birmingham B1 2RA
Tel: 0121 233 8733
Fax: 0121 233 8726
E-mail: neil.beasley@trinitypub.co.uk
Website: www.boatmark.co.uk

Boats and Planes For Sale
44a North Street
Chichester
West Sussex PO19 1NF
Tel: 01243 533394
Fax: 01243 532025
E-mail: sales@freedomhouse.co.uk
Website: www.boats-for-sale.com

Classic Boat
Link House
Dingwall Avenue
Croydon CR9 2TA
Tel: 020 8774 0603
Fax: 020 8774 0942
E-mail: cb@ipcmedia.com
Website: www.classicboat.co.uk

Motor Boat & Yachting
King's Reach Tower
Stamford Street
London SE1 9LS
Tel: 020 7261 5333
Fax: 020 7261 5419
E-mail: mby@ipcmedia.com
Website: www.mby.com

Motor Boats Monthly
King's Reach Tower
Stamford Street
London SE1 9LS
Tel: 020 7261 7256
Fax: 020 7261 7900
E-mail: mbm@ipcmedia.com
Website: www.motorboatsmonthly.co.uk

Power Boat Buyers' Guide
Shaftesbury House
22 Godesdone Road
Cambridge CB5 8HB
Tel: 01223 561156
Fax: 01223 471788

Practical Boat Owner
Westover House
West Quay Road
Poole
Dorset BH15 1JG
Tel: 01202 440820
Fax: 01202 440860
E-mail: pbo@ipc.co.uk
Website: www.pbo.co.uk

Sports Boat and Waterski International
CSL House
2a Tenison Road
Cambridge CB1 2DW
Tel: 01223 460490
Fax: 01223 576038
E-mail: gina@csl-pub.demon.co.uk
Website: www.sportsboat.co.uk

Waterways World
The Well House
High Street
Burton-on-Trent
Staffordshire DE14 1JQ
Tel: 01283 742950

Glossary of Terms

It is hardly surprising that mariners have built up their own vocabulary, because many parts of a boat and the methods of using them have no equivalent ashore.

Communication aboard is very important, so you must learn the more common terms in order that you can understand and be understood.

Abaft Behind; further aft than

Abeam On the beam; at right angles to the fore-and-aft line of the vessel

Aboard In or on the vessel; on board

A-bracket Fitting shaped as an inverted 'A' supporting the end of the propeller shaft

Adrift Loose; broken away; late

Afloat Waterborne

Aft Towards the stern

Ahead In front of: the direction of the bows

Amidships Midway between bow and stern; of the rudder or helm when it is centred (fore-and-aft)

Astern Behind: in the direction of the stern

Athwart Across

Avast Stop (eg 'Avast heaving' – stop heaving)

Awash Level with the surface of the water

Aweigh When the anchor has broken out of the sea bed

Bailer A receptacle for removing water from a boat (bailing)

Ballast Weight placed low down in a vessel to improve stability

Bar A shallow area (shoal) across the mouth of a harbour or a river

Beacon A mark to assist navigation

Beam The width of a boat; the timber on which the deck is laid

Bearing The direction of one object from another, usually referred to the compass

Bear off To push away from (eg the jetty or another boat)

Beaufort Scale A numerical measure of wind strength

Before Towards the bow

Belay To secure a rope, or make it fast (Colloquially, to countermand an order)

Bend A form of knot

Berth Space for sleeping, or for a vessel to dock

Bight The middle of a rope (not the ends)

Bilge The curve of the underwater part of a boat, between the waterline and the keel

Binnacle The casing that holds a compass

Bitts A pair of vertical posts for securing mooring lines or anchor warps

Bollard A vertical post on ship or shore, for securing mooring lines

Boot-topping Painted area along the waterline

Bow The front end of a vessel

Bowline A knot that forms a fixed loop

Bring up To come to anchor

Broach To swing broadside on to the sea

Bulkheads Vertical partitions or divisions within a vessel

Bulwarks Solid rails around the deck edge

Buoy A float used as a navigational mark, or to take a mooring line

Burgee A triangular flag denoting membership of a club, flown at the masthead

By the head A vessel trimmed bow down

By the stern A vessel trimmed stern down

Cable Anchor chain; or, as a measure of distance, $1/10$ of a nautical mile, ie about 200 yards

Careen To heel a vessel over to work on her bottom

Carry away To break or part

Carry way For a boat to continue to move through the water

Carvel A method of construction which gives a smooth finish, with planks edge to edge

Cast off To let go

Catamaran A vessel with two parallel hulls, joined by beams

Caulk To make a watertight joint in seams between planks

Cavitation Underwater vibration and loss of power, caused by aeration of propeller working surfaces

Centre of buoyancy Centre of the immersed volume of a vessel

Chart A nautical map

Chart datum The level against which soundings and drying heights on a chart are measured

Check (Of a rope) to ease out slowly; slowly to stop a vessel's movement

Chine The angle between the bottom and topsides in some designs of craft

Cleat A fitting for securing ropes

Clinker A method of construction where the edge of one plank overlaps the one below it

Coachroof A raised structure to improve headroom below deck

Companionway Ladder or stairway

Compass Navigational instrument which indicates magnetic north

Con To give orders to the helmsman

Counter The overhanging portion of the stern

Course The direction in which a vessel is heading

Crown (Of an anchor) where the arms join the shank

Crutch Metal holder that drops into gunwale of a boat to support an oar

Davits Cranes for hoisting boats and tenders

Dead reckoning Calculating position from course steered and distance run

Deck head Ceiling

Deviation Compass error caused by magnetic influence of the vessel eg engine, electrics

Dip To lower and re-hoist the ensign as a salute

Displacement The weight of a vessel (equal to the weight of water she displaces)

Dog watch The two two-hour watches from 1600-1800 and 1800-2000

Draft (or draught) The depth of a vessel beneath the water, to the lowest part of the hull or keel

Ebb The falling tide

Echo sounder Electronic instrument to measure the depth of water

Ensign A vessel's national flag. The British maritime flags are the red, white or blue ensigns (never the Union Flag)

Fairlead An opening or fining for leading a (mooring) rope

Fairway A navigable channel

Fathom An old fashioned measurement of depth, equalling six feet

Fender Used to prevent damage to the ship's side when lying alongside another vessel or a jetty

Fend off To push off

Fiddle A lip around horizontal surfaces to stop objects falling or sliding off

Fix A position found from accurate bearings or observations of heavenly bodies

Flood The rising tide

Forward Towards the bow

Foul Opposite to 'clear' eg 'foul anchor' 'foul bottom'

Founder To sink

Freeboard The height of the deck above the waterline

Gale Wind of force 8 or 9 on the Beaufort Scale (34-47 knots)

Galley The kitchen

Gimbals Two pivoted concentric rings that hold items such as compass or lamps level at sea

GPS Global Positioning System. Electronic system using satellites to give an accurate position.

101

Gunwale The upper edge along the side of a vessel

Halyard Rope or wire used to hoist a sail, or flag

Handsomely Gently or slowly

Hard A place for beaching boats

Hard a-port/hard a-starboard Helm orders to use maximum helm in required direction

Hatchway A deck opening with a cover (hatch)

Hawse pipe A hole or pipe below deck edge, through which the anchor cable runs

Heads The lavatory

Heave-to To stop or reduce speed with vessel head to wind

Heaving line A line with a weighted end for establishing contact with another vessel or shore

Heel The inclination of a vessel

Helm The tiller or wheel

Hitch To make a rope fast to an object (not another rope)

Holding ground The type of bottom for the anchor

House flag A rectangular, personal flag of owner

Hull The structure of a boat, to deck level

Inboard Towards the middle of a vessel

Inshore Towards the shore

Jury Makeshift

Kedge A light or secondary anchor

Keel The lower fore-and-aft structure of a vessel

King spoke The spoke of steering wheel upright when rudder is centred

Knot One nautical mile per hour (speed)

Landfall First sight of land, approaching from seaward

Lashing Securing with rope

Latitude Angular measurement of position north or south of equator

Launch To slip into the water

Lead line Weight on a marked line, used for finding depth of water

Leeward The side of vessel further from the wind (opposite to 'windward')

Lee shore Shore on to which wind is blowing

Leeway The sideways movement of a vessel, blown by the wind (to leeward)

Lifeline Line rigged to stop crew going overboard

List Angle of heel

Log Instrument for measuring distance run through the water

Log book Record of vessel's movements, positions, etc

Longitude Angular measurement east or west of Greenwich meridian

Loom The inboard end of an oar, of a light: reflection in the sky

Lubber's line Fixed mark on compass bowl, showing ship's head

Make To reach port; of tides: when range and strength are increasing (from neaps to springs)

Make water To leak

Making way Moving through the water

Man To provide a crew for a certain purpose (eg man the pump)

Meridian A north-south line through any point

Midships Midway between bow and stern; of the rudder or helm when it is centred (fore-and-aft)

Moor To anchor, or secure alongside a quay or pontoon

Neaps When the tide does not rise or fall very much (opposite of 'springs')

Nothing to port (or starboard) Do not steer any further to port (or starboard)

Overboard Over the side (into the water)

P-bracket Fitting shaped as an inverted 'P' supporting the end of the propeller shaft

Painter The rope secured to the bows of a dinghy or tender, by which it is secured or towed

Pay off To allow the ship's head to swing away from the direction of the wind

Pay out To ease out a chain or rope

Plotter Graphical position display which can be used in conjunction to overlay vessel's position onto graphically displayed chart

Pooped When a vessel is overtaken by a sea which breaks over the stern (poop)

Port (side) The left hand side of a vessel looking forward

Port tack When a sailing vessel has the wind blowing from her port side, and her main boom is to starboard

Quarter Midway between the beam and right aft

Race A local area of disturbed water

Radar Electronic instrument that shows the positions of other objects (ships, shore, buoys, etc)

Range (of cable) To flake down lengths of cable on deck, before anchoring (of tide) the difference in height between successive high and low waters

Rhumb line A course which cuts all meridians at the same angle (a straight line on a Mercator chart)

Riding light Anchor light

Rubbing strake A wood or rubber strip secured along the hull, that takes the wear alongside a jetty

Samson post Post for securing anchor or tow line

Scantlings The dimensions of a vessel's timbers (constructional details)

Scupper Holes in bulwarks to allow water to drain from deck

Scuttles Round openings in vessel's side, sometimes referred to as port holes

Seacock A valve on a pipe connected to the sea

Sheer The rising line of a vessel's side, towards bow and stern

Sheet Rope used to control a sail's angle to the wind

Ship To take on board

Shoal Shallow area of water

Shrouds Athwartships or lateral supports to mast

Slack water When the tidal stream is stationary

Sound To ascertain the depth

Spring Mooring rope led from forward aft, or from aft forward

Spring tide When the range of the tide is greatest (opposite of 'neaps')

Starboard The right hand side of the vessel looking forward

Starboard tack When a sailing vessel has the wind blowing from her starboard side, and her main boom is to port

Stay Fore-and-aft support for mast

Steady Order to helmsman to maintain the course he is steering

Steerage way When a vessel is moving fast enough through the water to respond to her helm

Stem The foremost part of the hull

Surge To allow a rope to slip round a winch or bollard

Tabernacle Deck fitting for the bottom of a mast which will allow it to be lowered

Tack To work a sailing vessel to windward by sailing alternately on port and starboard tacks

Thwart Seat running across (athwart) an open boat

Tidal stream The movement of the sea caused by the tide

Tide The periodic rise and fall in level of the sea caused by the gravitational attraction of the moon and sun

Tiller bar connected to the rudder for operating same

Topsides Surfaces of the hull above the waterline

Transom Flat stern of some designs of vessels

Turn up To make a rope fast

Under way When a vessel is not anchored or secured to the land or shore in any way

Up and down When the anchor cable is vertical

Veer To pay out anchor cable

VHF radio Very high frequency marine band radio system used for ship to ship and ship to shore communications from 5-40 miles range

Wake Disturbed water astern of a vessel as she moves ahead

Warp Rope used for mooring, anchoring or moving a vessel

Wash The waves caused by a vessel's progress through the water

Watches Periods of duty for members of the crew

Waypoint Predetermined position used in compiling a navigation route

Windward The side of a vessel nearer the wind (opposite to 'leeward')

Weigh To raise the anchor

Wind rode When a vessel is lying to the wind (rather than the tide)

Yaw To steer an unsteady course

Index